Bible Stories

The
GOLDEN PRESS
Classics Library

BIBLE STORIES

FROM THE OLD AND NEW TESTAMENTS

BASED ON THE STORY OF THE BIBLE BY CHARLES FOSTER

EDITED BY THEA HEINEMANN

ILLUSTRATED BY HUNTLEY BROWN

GOLDEN PRESS

Western Publishing Company, Inc., Racine, Wisconsin

Contents

Contents — Continued

Contents — Continued

The Garden of Eden

A VERY LONG WHILE ago, before anybody can remember, God made the world. Yet it did not look at first as it does now, for there was nothing living on it—no men or animals or birds; and there was nothing growing on it—no trees or bushes or flowers. It was all lonely and dark everywhere.

Then God made the light. He said, "Let there be light," and the light came. God saw the light and was pleased with it, and He gave the light a name; He called it Day. When the day was gone and the darkness came again to stay for a little while, He called that darkness Night. God did these things on the first day. And God saw that it was good.

God made the clouds, and He made the sky up above the world. He gave the sky a name; He called it Heaven. God did this on the second day.

And God saw that it was good.

God said that the waters should go into one place by themselves. When they had gone into that one place, and were very deep and wide there, God gave the waters a name; He called them Seas, and the dry land He called Earth. God made the grass to grow up out of the earth, and the bushes and the trees that have fruit on them. The grass and the bushes and the trees were to bear seeds so that when those seeds were planted in the ground more grass and more trees would grow there. God did these things on the third day.

And God saw that it was good.

God made two great lights, the sun to shine in the day and the moon to shine in the night. He made the stars, also. He set the sun and the moon and the stars up in the sky where we see them now. God did this on the fourth day.

He saw that it was good.

He made the great whales and all the fishes that swim about in the sea. He made the birds, also—some to fly over the water and swim upon it and live near it, like ducks and geese; and some to live all the time upon the land and in the woods, like eagles, robins, pigeons, and wrens. God made these on the fifth day.

And God saw this was good.

He made the animals—those that are wild and live out in the forest, such as the elephants, lions, tigers, and bears; and those that are tame and useful to men, and that live where men live, such as horses, oxen, cows, and sheep. He made the little insects that creep on the ground and the flies that fly in the air.

Then God said, "Let Us make Man in Our image, after Our likeness." When He had done this, God spoke kindly to man and told him that he should be master over the fish of the sea, the birds of the air, and over everything that was living on the earth. And God told man that the fruit which grew on the trees and on the bushes should be his food. The animals were given the grass and the leaves of the bushes to eat.

God looked at all the things He had made, and He was pleased with them. This was the sixth day.

The earth and the skies were finished in six days. The seventh day God rested from all His work, and the Bible tells us He sanctified the seventh day; that is, He separated it from the other days of the week and made it a holy day.

Now, we have been told how the earth and the skies were made; God made them. He made every bush and every tree, for there had been no rain to make them grow, and no man to plant them. After God had planted them, the trees, the bushes, and the grass took root in the soil and grew by themselves.

God made man out of the dust that lies on the ground. He breathed into him, and then the man breathed and moved and was alive, because God had breathed into him. The Lord God planted a garden for the man He had made; it was called the Garden of Eden. In that garden God made to grow every tree that was beautiful to look at and that bore fruit good to eat. A river flowed through the garden and watered it.

God took Adam, the man He made, and put him into the garden to take care of it. God told him he might eat of the fruit of every tree in the garden except one. That one was called the Tree of the Knowledge of Good and Evil. God said he must not eat of that tree, for if he did eat of it he should surely die.

God said it was not good that the man should be alone. Therefore, God made someone to be with him and help him. He caused Adam to fall into a deep sleep. While he was sleeping, God took out of his side a piece of bone, and of that bone He made a woman. And God brought the woman He had made to Adam, and she was his wife.

All the animals and the birds came to Adam; God sent

11

them to him that he might give them their names. Whatever Adam called each one was its name.

Now, there was a serpent in the Garden of Eden. The serpent spoke to the woman, not by itself, but by Satan, the wicked Spirit who comes into our hearts and tempts us to sin. The serpent asked her, "Has God said you shall not eat of every tree in the garden?"

The woman answered that they might eat of all the trees except one. Of that tree God had commanded them not to eat, lest they should die. The serpent told her they should not die, and that God had forbidden them to eat of the tree because it would make them wise.

The woman listened to what the serpent said, and when she saw that the tree was beautiful to look at and that the fruit seemed good to eat, remembering that the serpent had said it would make her wise, she took some of the fruit and ate of it. She also gave to her husband, and he ate, too.

After they had eaten they heard a voice in the garden. They knew it was God's voice, yet they did not come when they heard it. They were afraid and hid themselves among the trees.

God spoke again. He called to Adam, saying, "Where art thou?"

Adam answered, "I heard Thy voice in the garden, and I was afraid and hid myself."

God said, "Hast thou eaten of the tree I commanded thee not to eat of?"

Then Adam began to make excuse. He blamed the woman, saying, "The woman whom Thou gavest to be with me, she gave me of the fruit, and I did eat."

God said to the woman, "What is this that thou hast done?"

The woman answered, "The serpent deceived me, and I did eat."

God was angry with Adam and the woman, and with

the serpent, also. The serpent, He said, should be punished by having to crawl on the ground with its mouth in the dust all the days of its life. He told the woman, also, that she should have sickness and sorrow. God drove Adam and his wife out of the beautiful garden; He would let them live there no longer. He sent cherubim, or angels, that kept watch, and a fiery sword that turned every way, to prevent them from going into the garden again. To Adam God said that, because he had listened to his wife's voice and eaten of the tree which the Lord commanded him not to eat of, the ground should not anymore bear fruit for him by itself, without his labor, as it used to do in the Garden of Eden, but it should send up thorns and thistles; Adam would have to work very hard as long as he lived to raise food to eat. When he should die, God said, his body would go back to dust again, like the dust out of which the Lord had made him.

Adam gave his wife a name; he called her Eve. And God made coats for them out of the skins of animals.

After a while, Adam and Eve had children. When they grew up, they had children. When those children grew up, they had children, and soon there were many people in the land.

Two Brothers
Give Thanks to God

CAIN AND ABEL were brothers. They were the sons of Adam and Eve, the first people in the world. They were grown men in this story told about them in the Bible.

Cain took care of the land and raised good things to eat. He worked hard tending to his garden. God sent rain and sunshine and made the ground to give rich foods.

Abel was a keeper of sheep. Each day he took them to green pastures to eat good grass. Abel carefully watched over his sheep. God kept them in good health and from all harm and danger. There were many fine sheep in the fold that belonged to Abel.

Both Cain and Abel knew that God had cared for them. To show their thanks, they gave Him a present.

Each brother took a pile of stone and built a fire in the center of the pile. Abel chose the finest lamb from

14

his fold and laid it on the fire.

"I hope this gift will please God," said Abel, "for I want Him to know how glad I am that He has taken care of me."

Cain took some grains from his garden and placed them on his fire as his gift. Deep down in his heart, though, he did not really feel thankful for God's care. He was giving because he felt he should.

The Bible tells us that God watched the two brothers at their fires. He was angry with Cain because his gift was not given with a truly thankful heart. He was pleased with Abel because he gave his lamb gladly.

Noah's Ark

WHEN THERE CAME to be many more people living in the world, they grew very wicked. Their hearts were filled with sinful thoughts and all their acts were evil, for they did not care to please God or even try to obey Him. Therefore, God was angry with them. He said He would punish them by sending a flood that should cover the earth with deep water and drown all the people, the animals, the birds, and everything that lived upon the ground. Almost all the people in the world were very wicked. Not quite all, however. There was one good man, and his name was Noah. The Bible tells us he was a just man, and that he walked with God. Therefore, God loved Noah and told him of the flood He was going to send.

God commanded Noah to build a great houseboat called an ark. It was to be very large, with rooms in it, and a window and a great door in its side, and was to be three stories high.

God told Noah that when the ark was finished he and his sons and their wives should go into it. He commanded Noah to take in with him some of every kind of beast, bird, and insect. He was to keep them alive while the flood should be on the earth, for all that were not in the ark would be drowned.

Then Noah began to build the ark. It took him a great while to build it. Noah not only worked at building the ark—the Bible says he was a preacher. He spoke to the people about God and about the punishment that was coming upon them for their sins. They would not repent, nor believe what he told them, however, so Noah had to hear their wicked words and see their wicked acts all the time he was building the ark. Yet he worked patiently, until at last he finished it as God had commanded him.

Then God spoke to Noah and told him to come with all his family into the ark, for He had observed him to be a good man among all those wicked men who were living on the earth. God told Noah to bring the birds and the beasts also with him into the ark, for in seven days He would send the rain on the earth, and everything that was living on the dry land would be drowned. Noah did as God commanded. He went with his wife and his three sons and their wives into the ark. He took the beasts, birds, and insects in with him. When they were all safe inside the ark, God shut them in.

After seven days the rain began, and it rained without stopping for forty days and forty nights. The Bible says the windows of heaven were opened. This means that the rain came down not only in little drops, as we know it, but it came down as if poured out of great windows up in the sky. The springs, the creeks, the rivers, and the great ocean all began to rise up and overflow the land. After a while the water surrounded the ark. It rose higher and

higher till the ark floated and was lifted up from the place where Noah had been building it so long. The ground everywhere began to be covered with water.

God remembered Noah and took care of him and of those who were with him through all that dreadful storm. He kept the ark safe till the rain stopped and the waters began to flow back again into the seas and rivers and springs underground, where they were before the flood.

After Noah had been in the ark a hundred and fifty days, the waters were gone down so much that the ark rested on the top of a mountain called Ararat. There it stood, resting on the top of the mountain, for more than two months. By that time the waters were lower still, and the tops of other mountains could be seen peeping above them.

Noah opened the window of the ark and let a raven go. The raven flew about over the water and roosted at night on the tops of the mountains or on the roof of the ark, but never came back to Noah again.

Then Noah sent out another bird. It was a dove. He sent it that it might fly off and see whether the waters had left the ground dry yet. But they had not left it dry. Although the tops of the mountains were not covered, the rest of the ground was. The dove found no pleasant place with trees and flowers where she would like to stay, so she came back to the window of the ark. Noah put out his hand and took her in.

Noah waited seven days longer and sent her out again. In the evening she came back to him as before, but this time with a leaf in her mouth, plucked from an olive tree. When Noah saw the leaf, he knew that the waters must have gone down greatly or the dove could not have found it. God had taught the dove to pluck that leaf and carry it to Noah so that he might know the ground would soon be dry. Noah waited another seven days and sent the dove forth once more. This time she did not come back to him.

By now, no doubt, the woods were pleasant to fly about in, much pleasanter than the ark where the dove had been shut up for so long.

Noah looked and saw that the ground was dry. God spoke to him and told him to come out of the ark and to bring out his wife and his sons and their wives, and the beasts, birds, and insects that had been in the ark with him. So Noah came out and brought every living thing, and they walked on the dry ground. Noah built an altar and offered up animals and birds upon it to the Lord, who had saved him and his family from the flood while all the other people in the world were drowned.

God spoke kindly to Noah and his sons. He said they should be masters over everything living on the earth, and that they might kill the animals for food. He had given Adam only the fruits which grew on the trees and the bushes for food. Now, after the flood, He said that men might kill and eat any animal they chose.

God promised that He would never send another flood over the earth to drown all the people as this one had done. And He gave Noah a token to make him remember and believe God's promise, so that he need never be afraid of a flood anymore. This token was a beautiful thing, and God set it up in the sky where Noah could often see it. As often as he saw it Noah thought of God's promise. The token that God gave Noah was the rainbow.

Even today, after a heavy rain, we can sometimes look up in the sky and see the rainbow. We, too, can remember God's promise to Noah and to all the people forever after, that He would never again send a flood like the one in those long-ago days.

The Tower of Babel

GOD GAVE TO Noah's sons children of their own. When they grew up, they had children, too, so that after a while there came to be a great many people on earth once more.

There was only one language in the world then. The people all talked alike and could all understand each other.

Once as they journeyed from the east they came to a plain in the land of Shinar. They stopped there.

They said one to another, "Let us make brick and build a city and a tower whose top may reach up to heaven." They wanted to build a city so that they would never be separated but could live together always. And so they began to build.

The Lord came down from heaven to see the city and tower which the people were building. When He saw them, He was displeased. He did something to stop them then. He made the people, all at once, begin to speak in different languages, such as they had never spoken before. They could not go on building because they were not able to understand each other's words. Therefore, they had to cease building before the tower was done.

After that they would not wish to live together anymore. Only those who talked the same language would want to live together, and they would go off to some place where they could be by themselves. This is the way that people, at first, were separated from one another and came to live in different parts of the world.

The tower which they tried to build, but which God would not allow them to finish, was called the tower of Babel. Babel means *confusion.*

Hagar and Ishmael

THERE WAS A man who lived in the land whose name was Abraham. He had a wife whose name was Sarah. For a long time Abraham and Sarah had wanted a son. God promised that He would send one, for Abraham had been faithful to Him for many years. In due time the baby was born, and Sarah and Abraham rejoiced greatly. They called his name Isaac as God had commanded them.

Hagar, a servant in Abraham's household, also had a son. His name was Ishmael.

Once when Isaac was a little boy, Abraham made him a feast. Ishmael was invited to the feast. Sarah saw Ishmael mocking Isaac, and she was displeased with Ishmael. She asked Abraham to send him and his mother away. But Abraham did not wish to send them away, and it troubled him when Sarah asked him to do this.

HAGAR AND ISHMAEL

God spoke to Abraham and told him to do as Sarah had said. So he rose up early in the morning, took food and a bottle of water, and gave them to Hagar, Ishmael's mother.

The bottles of that country were what we would call canteens or bags. They were made of goatskins, folded over and sewed tightly together around the edges, except at the neck, which was left open for the water to pass through. When Abraham had given Hagar the food and the bottle of water, he sent her and her son away.

Hagar took her boy and went into the wilderness. When all the water in the bottle was gone, and they had no more to drink, the boy grew weak. Hagar thought he would die, and so she laid him in the shade under a bush and went a little way off and sat down and wept, for she did not want to see the lad die.

God heard her weeping, and the angel of God called to her out of heaven and said, "What aileth thee, Hagar?" Then the angel told her not to be afraid, but to lift up Ishmael from the place where she had laid him and to hold him in her arms. God then showed her a well of water that was there in the wilderness. She went to it and filled the bottle and gave her son drink, and he became strong and well again.

God was kind to Ishmael after that, and he grew and lived in the wilderness and was an archer.

Abraham and Isaac

GOD HAD BEEN very good to Abraham. And Abraham loved God and tried to please Him. God wanted to prove this love, so one day God spoke to Abraham and said, "Abraham."

Abraham answered, "Here am I."

Then God said, "Take now thy son, thine only son Isaac, whom thou lovest, and get thee into the land of Moriah, and offer him there for a burnt offering upon one of the mountains which I will tell thee of."

Yes, Abraham was commanded to offer up Isaac upon an altar as if he had been a lamb. How could Abraham do this? God had told him to do it; Abraham had heard Him speak. Abraham knew that he should do whatever God said.

So Abraham rose up early in the morning and saddled

an ass. He took with him Isaac, two young men who were his servants, and the wood, ready cut to lay on the altar. Then he started out for the mountain of which God had told him. He journeyed that day and the next, and did not come to the place; but the following day, he looked up and saw it a good way off.

Abraham told the young men they need go no farther, for he did not wish them to see him offer up his son. He and Isaac, Abraham said, would go to the mountain and worship and come back to them again. Then he and Isaac went off together. Isaac carried the wood, and Abraham took some fire to light the wood, and he carried a knife in his hand.

Now, Isaac did not know what God had commanded his father to do or why his father was taking him to the mountain. He knew they were going to offer up a burnt offering, for they had wood to burn it with, and the knife to kill it, but he did not know that he was to be that burnt offering himself. As they walked together, he said to his father, "My father, I see the fire and the wood, but where is the lamb for a burnt offering?"

Abraham answered, "My son, God will find Himself a lamb for a burnt offering."

They came to the place which God had spoken of. There Abraham built an altar and laid the wood on it. He bound Isaac and laid him on the wood; then he put out his hand and took hold of the knife to kill his son. But just then the angel of the Lord called to him out of heaven, saying, "Abraham, Abraham."

He answered, "Here am I."

And the angel told him not to hurt Isaac, for now he knew that Abraham loved God, because he was willing to offer up his only son when God commanded him. Abraham looked and saw behind him a ram caught fast in the bushes by its horns. God had sent it there for a burnt offering instead of Isaac. Abraham took it and killed it

27

and offered it up on the altar.

God was pleased with Abraham. The angel of the Lord spoke to Abraham again out of heaven, telling him that because he had obeyed God and had been willing to offer up his son, God would bless him. The angel promised him that his descendants should be like the grains of sand on the seashore—so many of them that no one can count them.

The angel said to him, also, "In thy seed shall all the nations of the earth be blessed." This meant that the Savior whom God had promised should be descended from Abraham. So Abraham and Isaac returned to where the young men were waiting, and they all went back together to Beersheba where Abraham lived.

Isaac and Rebekah

W HEN ISAAC WAS grown up to be a man, Abraham, his father, did not wish him to take a wife from the women who lived in the land of Canaan, for they worshipped idols. He wanted Isaac to have his wife from that country where Abraham used to live, and where he had relatives still living who loved the Lord.

Now, that country was a long way from Canaan, so Abraham called his oldest servant, who took care of his silver and gold, his flocks and his herds, and all that he had, and asked him to promise that he would go to that country and bring back from there a wife for Isaac. The servant said that perhaps the woman would not be willing to come. Abraham told him that God would send an angel before him to help him and that he would be able to find a wife for Isaac there. If the woman should not be willing to come, Abraham said, he would excuse the servant from his promise. The servant promised to do as Abraham commanded.

So he took ten of Abraham's camels and some beautiful presents, and he went on his journey to the land where Abraham had sent him. When he came near to a city in that land, he made his camels kneel down by a well of water that was just outside the city. Camels were used in that country to ride upon, as we ride on horses. They carried heavy loads on their backs, also, and went a long way without resting. Before they started upon a journey they knelt down to have their loads put on them, and when they came to the end of a journey, they knelt down to have their packs taken off again.

It was evening, the time when women of that city came out to draw water from the well. Abraham's servant prayed that God would help him and make him know which of those young women that came to draw water should be Isaac's wife. But how would the servant know? In this way: He was going to ask one of them to give him some water from her pitcher. If she answered him kindly and said, "Drink, and I will give your camels drink, also," then she was to be the one whom God had chosen for Isaac's wife. But if she answered unkindly and would give him no water from her pitcher, she was not the one.

While he was praying, a beautiful young woman named Rebekah came out of the city, carrying her pitcher upon her shoulder. She went down to the well and filled it with water and came up again.

The servant ran to meet her and said, "Let me drink a little water out of your pitcher."

She answered, "Drink, and I will draw water for your camels, also."

She let down her pitcher from her shoulder and gave the man drink. Then she ran to the well and drew water for the camels, and they drank, too. The servant stood still,

wondering whether she was the one whom God had chosen to be Isaac's wife.

After the camels had finished drinking, the man took an earring of gold and two bracelets of gold and gave them to Rebekah. Then he asked whose daughter she was and whether there was room at her father's house for him and the men who were with him to sleep there. Rebekah told him that she was the daughter of Bethuel and that they had room at their house, and food and straw for the camels, too.

When the servant heard that she was Bethuel's daughter, he knew she was one of Abraham's relatives. He was glad and bowed down his head and worshipped the Lord, thanking Him for helping him find his master's relatives who lived so far away.

Rebekah left the servant and ran to her home and told her mother about all these things. She had a brother whose name was Laban. When Laban heard what she said and saw the earring and the bracelets, he ran out of the city to the man. He found him standing by his camels at the well. Laban asked him to come to their house; he said he had made it ready for him and that there was room for the camels. The man went with Laban, and Laban helped him to unload the camels. He gave him straw and food for the camels, and water for the men to wash their feet. Afterward there was food set before Abraham's servant that he might eat. But he said he would not eat until he had told them why he had come to their country.

Then he said he was Abraham's servant and that the Lord had blessed Abraham and made him great. He had given him silver and gold, and flocks, and herds, and camels, and asses. Best of all, He had given him a son. All his riches, the servant said, Abraham had given to his son Isaac. He told them that Abraham had sent him into their country to find a wife for Isaac. He had come to the well that day, praying that he would know which young woman was to be Isaac's wife. While he was praying, he said, Rebekah came out, and when he asked her for a drink, she answered him kindly, saying, "Drink, and I will give your camels drink, also."

Then the servant asked them whether they would let Rebekah go home with him to be Isaac's wife. They answered that it was the Lord who had done all these things; Rebekah might go.

When the servant heard this he was glad. He bowed himself down to the ground and worshipped the Lord. Afterward he brought out more beautiful presents—jewels of silver, jewels of gold, and raiment—and gave them to Rebekah. He gave her mother and her brother presents, also. Then he did eat and drink, he and the men that were with him, and they stayed at Laban's house all night.

When they rose up in the morning, Abraham's servant wanted to take Rebekah and go on his way back to the land of Canaan. But her mother and her brother did not wish to part with her so soon. They said, "Let her stay with us a few days, at least ten. After that she shall go."

Abraham's servant begged them not to detain him, because, he said, the Lord had helped him to do what his master sent him for, and he wanted to make haste home to his master again.

They said, "We will call Rebekah and ask her." They called her and asked, "Will you go with this man?"

She answered, "I will go." So they sent away Rebekah, and her nurse went with her, and they rode on the camels after Abraham's servant.

They came into the land of Canaan toward evening, about the time the sun goes down. Isaac had gone out into the field to walk there and think by himself. Perhaps he wondered whether the servant would soon be back, and whether the Lord had helped him find the woman who should be his wife. Isaac looked up and saw the camels were coming.

As they came nearer, Rebekah saw Isaac, and she asked the servant what man it was walking in the field to meet them. The servant told her it was Isaac. Then she took a veil and covered her face with it and came down from the camel. Isaac brought her into the tent that used to be his mother's, for his mother was dead. He took Rebekah and she was his wife, and he loved her.

Jacob and Esau

God was very kind to Isaac and blessed him. He gave Isaac and Rebekah two sons, Jacob and Esau. Esau was the elder, and Jacob was the younger.

Now, in those days the eldest son in every family had what was called the birthright. This made him the chief among all the children. He was greater than any of the others. When his father died he got more of the silver and gold and cattle that had been his father's than the others did. He got twice as much as any of them, because he had the birthright.

Esau was Isaac's eldest son, and, therefore, he had the birthright.

When Esau and Jacob grew up to be men, Esau was a hunter. He went out into the fields and woods, and killed deer, and brought the meat home to his father because his father loved to eat it. But Jacob lived at home in a tent and helped to take care of his father's flocks. One day Jacob had food called pottage. Esau came in from his hunting very weary and faint, and he asked Jacob to give him his pottage. Jacob told him he would do so if Esau would sell him his birthright. Then Esau, because he felt weak and sick, said that he was going to die and that the birthright would do him no good, so he sold it to Jacob. Jacob gave him the pottage for it. It was wrong for Esau to sell his birthright. God had given it to him, and he should not have sold it. It was wrong for Jacob, also, to take it from his brother.

Now, Isaac was old and could not see. He called Esau and told him to take his bow and go into the field and hunt a deer and cook the meat in the way that Isaac loved, and then bring it to him that he might eat of it.

Then, Isaac said, he would bless Esau before he died; that is, he would ask God to be kind to him and would tell Esau of the things he should have after his father was dead. For Isaac meant to bless Esau before he blessed Jacob, and to give him the best things, because Esau was his eldest son and had the birthright. Esau went out into the field to hunt deer for his father.

When Rebekah heard what Isaac said, she was not pleased, for she did not wish Esau to be blessed first, although he was the oldest son. She wished Jacob to be blessed first, because she loved him the best of her children.

So, after Esau had gone for the venison, she told Jacob to go to the flock and bring her two little kids. When he brought them, she cooked them, making nice food of them that tasted like the venison which his father loved. Then she put on Jacob some of Esau's clothes that were in the house and told him to take the food to his father, and to say it was Esau who brought it.

So Jacob came to his father with the food which his

mother had cooked. When his father asked who it was, Jacob said it was Esau and that he had brought the venison which his father told him to bring. Isaac could not see, so he put his hands on Jacob and felt the clothes and believed it was Esau. He then ate of the meat and blessed Jacob. It was wicked for Jacob to do this, and for his mother to help him, for although Esau sold him his birthright, Jacob should not have deceived his father.

As soon as Isaac had finished blessing Jacob, Esau came in from his hunting with the venison he had killed. And Isaac said to him, "Who is it?"

Esau answered, "I am Esau, your oldest son."

Isaac was surprised and afraid, and he trembled a great deal and asked who was it that had been there before and brought venison and taken Esau's blessing. Then Isaac knew it must have been Jacob, and he told Esau that his brother had been there before him and had taken away his blessing.

Esau was in great trouble. He cried with a loud voice and begged his father to bless him, also. Isaac did bless him, but he had promised the best things to Jacob and now he could not take them from him.

Jacob's Dream

JACOB HAD LEFT his home where his mother and father
lived. He left because his father told him to go to his
uncle's place in the east.

Jacob had walked all day. The sun was setting, and he
was getting tired, so he decided to stop for the night. Jacob
found some stones and used them as a pillow, and soon he
fell asleep.

While he was sleeping, he had a dream. He dreamed he
saw a ladder reaching up to heaven. Angels of God walked
up and down the ladder. And, behold, God stood at the
top of the ladder.

God spoke to Jacob and told him many things. He said
He would give him the land of Canaan and that his
descendants should be a great multitude of people. The
Lord said, too, that He would be with Jacob to take care

of him wherever he should go. And He promised to bring him back to his father's house again.

Early in the morning Jacob awoke from his sleep. He remembered the dream he had had in the night and he knew that God had surely spoken to him and would take care of him as He had promised.

Jacob knew, then, that the place where he had slept was a hallowed place. So he took the stones he had used for a pillow and stood them on end. Then he poured some oil on top of them. That is the way people showed their thanks to God a long time ago.

Then Jacob made a vow to God. Jacob promised that if the Lord would take care of him and give him food to eat and clothes to wear and keep him from harm, so that he should come back safely to his father's house again, then he would obey the Lord. He promised that of all the silver and gold, the flocks and the herds, which God should give him, he would give a tenth of it to the Lord.

Jacob and Rachel

Jacob went on his journey until he came near to Haran, where Laban, his uncle, lived. And he saw there a well in a field, with shepherds and three flocks of sheep lying down by it. A great stone was rolled over the mouth of the well to cover it. When all the flocks had come in from feeding, the shepherds would roll the stone away and draw up water for the sheep.

After they were done drinking, the stone was rolled back again over the mouth of the well.

Jacob asked the shepherds where their home was. They said it was at Haran.

"Do you know Laban?" Jacob asked.

They answered, "We know him." Jacob then asked if he was well.

They said, "He is well, and look, Rachel, his daughter,

is coming now with the sheep."

While they were speaking, Rachel came with her father's sheep, for she took care of them. Jacob went near and rolled away the stone and watered the flock for her. He kissed Rachel and told her he was her relative and Rebekah's son, and she ran and told her father.

When Laban heard that his sister Rebekah's son had come, he made haste and ran out to meet him. He put his arms around him and kissed him and brought him to his house. Laban spoke kindly to Jacob, and Jacob stayed at his house for a month.

Then Laban asked Jacob how much he should pay him to stay and live there and take care of his flock.

Now, Laban had another daughter beside Rachel, whose name was Leah, but Rachel was more beautiful than Leah.

Jacob loved Rachel, and he told Laban he would stay and serve him for seven years if, after they were ended, Rachel might be his wife. Laban said she might be. Therefore, Jacob served Laban seven years for her, and they seemed like only a few days to him because of the love he felt for her.

When they were ended, however, Laban would not give Rachel to Jacob, because she was the youngest. He gave him Leah and said that Jacob must serve seven more years for Rachel, for the youngest, he said, must not be married before the oldest. So Jacob stayed and served Laban seven years longer, and he had both Leah and Rachel for his wives. And God gave sons to him.

After this Jacob asked permission of Laban to take his wives and his children and go back to the land of Canaan. He wanted to see his father and mother, if they were still alive, and he thought perhaps that after so long a time Esau would forgive the unkindness he had done him when he took away his blessing.

Laban was not willing to let Jacob go. He had found, he said, that the Lord blessed him because Jacob was with

him, and he asked what wages he should give Jacob to stay longer. Jacob said that if Laban would give him some of the cattle which he took care of, he would stay and feed his flock as he had done before. Therefore, Laban gave Jacob some of his cattle, and he stayed and took care of Laban's flock.

Then Jacob had sheep and goats of his own. These he kept separate from Laban's and put them in a different place. It took three days to go from Laban's flock to the place where Jacob kept his flock. Jacob's flock grew to be a great many, so that after a while he was rich and had herds of cattle, and his sons took care of them. And Jacob had menservants and maidservants, and camels and asses.

One day Jacob heard Laban's sons speaking unkindly of him. They said he had taken away their father's cattle, and that was the reason he had grown so rich. Jacob saw that Laban did not look on him as kindly as he used to. His face was changed and he looked displeased whenever he spoke to Jacob.

The Lord spoke to Jacob and commanded him to go back to the land of his fathers; that is, to the land of Canaan, where Abraham, his grandfather, had lived when he was alive, and where Isaac, his father, was living still. The Lord said He would be with Jacob to take care of him and keep him from harm. Then Jacob called Rachel and Leah to him while he was out in the field with his flock. He wanted to talk with them there so that Laban could not hear what he said. When they came he told them that their father did not look as kindly on him as he used to, and that the Lord had commanded him to go back to Canaan. Rachel and Leah told him to do as the Lord commanded.

Jacob made ready to go. He set his wives and his children upon camels and took all his cattle and everything that belonged to him and started on his journey toward the land of Canaan. But Laban had gone away from his home to shear his sheep, and he did not know when Jacob left, because Jacob had kept it a secret from him. On the third day after Jacob had gone, someone told Laban of it. Then Laban took men with him and followed after Jacob. No doubt he was angry and wanted to do him some harm, but in a dream God spoke to Laban and told him not to harm Jacob nor speak unkindly to him. Laban did not overtake Jacob until he had been following him seven days, for Jacob had gone a long way, across a river and through a wide lonely country, to a mountain called Gilead. There Laban came up with him.

Now, Jacob had set up his tent at Mount Gilead. When Laban came there he set up a tent, also. Laban asked Jacob why he had gone away secretly and carried Rachel and Leah and their children with him, without letting Laban know, for, Laban said, Jacob had not allowed him to kiss his sons and his daughters before they went. Jacob answered that he had gone away secretly because he was afraid Laban would take Rachel and Leah from him if Laban knew of his going. Jacob was displeased at Laban for coming after him and asked Laban why he had followed him.

Jacob said that he had served Laban for twenty years, taking care of his sheep and his goats. He had been out in the night and in the day, when it was cold and when it was hot, watching over them. Now, he said, if God had not been with him to help him, Laban would have sent him away without giving him anything for the work he had done.

Then Laban spoke kindly to Jacob and said, "Your wives and your children are the same to me as if they were my own, and I would not do them any harm. Let us, therefore, be friends and make a covenant together."

They piled up stones and made a heap of them in that place and promised they would do each other no harm.

That heap was always there to remind them of the covenant they had made. If ever they should be angry and want to harm each other, when they came to that heap and saw the stones there, they would remember their covenant and turn back.

Jacob built an altar and offered up a sacrifice on Mount Gilead, and he and Laban and the men who were with him ate bread together. They stayed all night at the mount. Early in the morning Laban rose up and kissed Rachel and Leah and their children and blessed them and then went back to his own home.

Joseph and His Coat of Many Colors

ONCE THERE WAS a boy named Joseph. He was a good lad and much loved by his father, Jacob.

One day Joseph's father gave him a beautiful coat of many colors. The young boy was proud and happy to wear the cloak. He knew that it had been given to him to show the great love that his father had for him. Whenever he wore his bright-colored coat he felt happy. Joseph knew that his father wanted to keep him safe, just as the coat kept him warm.

Now, Joseph had eleven brothers, and none of them had a coat as beautiful as Joseph's.

When the ten older brothers saw Joseph's coat of many colors, they were jealous. They did not like it that their father had given him a new coat and had not given each of them something. They were angry and began to quarrel bitterly with their younger brother.

One day Jacob sent his older sons to a place far from home. They were to take their flocks to graze in fields there.

After a while Jacob became concerned about the boys. He called to Joseph and said, "Your brothers are feeding flocks in Shechem. Will you go there and see if they are all well?"

"Yes, Father," said the boy. "I will go." So Joseph went in search of his brothers.

The brothers saw Joseph coming across the field wearing his coat of many colors.

"Let us kill him and put him in a pit," they said.

The oldest brother, Reuben, did not like the idea. "We must not kill Joseph," he said, "but let us put him in the pit and leave him there." Reuben planned to help Joseph out of the pit when the others were not looking and send him back home to his father.

As he hurried toward them, Joseph did not know that his brothers had been plotting against him. He did not understand why they seized him and took away his fine new coat of many colors, then took him and put him into a pit.

The brothers then sat down to eat their food. But, looking up, they saw some men, called Ishmaelites, coming toward them with their camels. These men were merchants—men who carried things to sell—and they were going down into Egypt. When Judah, another of Joseph's brothers, saw them, he asked what good there would be in killing Joseph. "Come, let us sell him to the Ishmaelites," he said, and his brothers agreed.

When the Ishmaelites with their camels came by, Joseph's brothers lifted him out of the pit and sold him for twenty pieces of silver. The Ishmaelites took him and carried him down into Egypt. But Reuben, the one who had wanted to take Joseph back to his father, was not there when his brothers sold him. Afterward he went to the pit to find Joseph and when he could not, he was greatly distressed.

Then Joseph's brothers took his coat and killed a kid and dipped the coat in its blood. They brought it to their father and told him they found it. He could tell, they said, whether it was Joseph's coat or not. Jacob knew it and said, "It is my son's coat. An evil beast has devoured him. Joseph is, without doubt, torn in pieces."

So Jacob rent his clothes and put on sackcloth, a dark, coarse kind of cloth which persons wore to show they were in trouble. Jacob was in great trouble for many days. No one could persuade him to stop mourning, for he said that he would mourn till he should go down into the grave to Joseph. He meant, until he himself should die.

Joseph in Egypt

THE ISHMAELITES BROUGHT Joseph down into Egypt. The king of that country was named Pharaoh, and he had an officer in his army whose name was Potiphar. Potiphar bought Joseph, and Joseph was Potiphar's servant and lived in his house. The Lord helped Joseph in serving his master. His master was greatly pleased with Joseph and set him over his other servants. Joseph had the care of his house and of everything in it, for his master trusted Joseph with all that he had. The Lord blessed Potiphar because Joseph was with him.

After a while Potiphar's wife persuaded her husband that Joseph was a wicked man. Potiphar took Joseph and put him in prison. But the Lord was kind to Joseph. He made the keeper of the prison his friend, so that he set Joseph over the other prisoners as Potiphar had set Joseph over the other servants. The keeper gave the care of all the men in the prison to Joseph; he did not watch over them any longer. The Lord helped Joseph to do all things well.

Two of Pharaoh's servants offended him. One was his chief baker, who attended to cooking his food, and the other was his chief butler, who carried his wine cup to him when he wanted to drink. Pharaoh was displeased with them both and put them into the prison where Joseph was, and Joseph had the care of them there. Each of these men dreamed a dream on the same night. When Joseph came in to them in the morning, he saw they looked sad.

He asked them, "Why do you look so sad today?"

They answered, "We have dreamed a dream, and there is no interpreter of it." They meant there was no one to explain the dream, for an interpreter is a person who explains to us something which we do not understand. Joseph asked the men if God could not interpret all things, and he told them to tell him their dreams.

So the chief butler told his dream to Joseph. He said that he thought he saw a vine, and on the vine were three branches. While he was looking, buds appeared on the branches, and very soon these buds changed into bunches of ripe grapes. The butler thought he was holding Pharaoh's wine cup in his hand, so he took the grapes and pressed the juice out of them into the cup and gave the cup to Pharaoh that he might drink. This was the chief butler's dream.

Joseph interpreted it for him, for God showed Joseph what the dream meant. He said the three branches which the butler saw on the vine meant three days, and within three days Pharaoh would take him out of prison and bring him to the king's house again. There he should wait on the king and give the cup into his hand, as he used to do when he was butler before. Then Joseph asked the chief butler to remember him when he should come to the king's house and to speak to Pharaoh about him so that he might be brought out of the prison, because, Joseph said, he had been stolen away from the land of the Hebrews—that is, the land of Canaan—and since he had been in Egypt he had not done anything that they should put him in prison for.

When the chief baker saw that the butler's dream meant something good, he told Joseph his dream. He said that he thought he was carrying three baskets on his head, one above the other. In the highest basket were all kinds of cooked meats for Pharaoh, and the birds flew down and ate the meats out of the basket. Then Joseph told him the meaning: The three baskets meant three days.

"Within three days," he said, "Pharaoh shall hang you on a tree, and the birds shall eat your flesh."

It came true as Joseph said. In three days it was the king's birthday, and he made a feast to all his servants. He sent and brought the chief butler back to his house again, so that he gave the wine cup into Pharaoh's hand as he used to do when he was butler before. And Pharaoh hanged the chief baker as Joseph had foretold.

But the chief butler, when he was taken back to the king's house, forgot all about Joseph and did not speak to Pharaoh about him.

After Joseph had been in prison two whole years, Pharaoh dreamed a dream. He thought he stood by the river that was in Egypt and saw seven cows come up out of the water. They were fat and well-looking, and they went into a meadow and ate the grass there. After them came up seven other cows, but these were thin and starved-looking. The thin and starved-looking cows ate up those that were fat and well-looking. Then Pharaoh awoke.

He slept and dreamed again. He thought he saw seven ears of corn grow upon one stalk. They were all good and filled with grain. And after them came up seven bad ears that were spoiled and had no good grain in them. The seven bad ears ate up the seven good ones. And Pharaoh awoke and found it was a dream.

In the morning he was troubled and sent for all the wise men of Egypt and told them his dreams, but they could not interpret them. Then the chief butler spoke and said that he remembered something from when Pharaoh was angry with him and with the chief baker and put them both into prison. Each of them had had a dream one night, and a young man who was in the prison interpreted their dreams, and what that young man told them came true.

Then Pharaoh sent for Joseph. They brought him quickly out of prison, and he shaved himself and put on other clothes and came to Pharaoh.

Pharaoh said to Joseph, "I have dreamed a dream, and none can interpret it. I have heard that you can understand a dream and interpret it."

Joseph answered that it was not he, but God, who would tell Pharaoh the things he wanted to know. Pharaoh told Joseph his dreams. He told about the one in which he thought he stood by the bank of the river and saw the seven bad cows eat up the seven good ones, and after they had eaten them, no person could have told they had eaten anything, for they were as thin and starved-looking as before. Pharaoh told Joseph his dream about the ears of corn, also.

Joseph said that the king's dreams both meant the same thing, and that God had showed Pharaoh in these dreams what He was going to do. The seven good cows and the seven good ears of corn, he said, meant seven years; and the seven bad cows and the seven bad ears of corn meant seven other years. First there would come seven good years in Egypt, when the corn would grow well and there would be plenty for the people to eat. After those seven good years would come seven bad years, when the people would want bread because there would be a famine.

Joseph told Pharaoh to look for some wise man who

could attend to saving up the corn for him in the seven good years, so that when the bad years should come the people would have bread to eat and not starve. The king was willing to do as Joseph told him. He said that as God had taught Joseph how to interpret his dreams and showed him all these things which were to happen, Joseph was the wisest man. Joseph would save the corn for him.

So Pharaoh would not let Joseph go back to prison anymore, but he made him a great man. He took off his ring from his hand and put it on Joseph's hand and dressed him in rich clothing and put a gold chain about his neck. He made him ride also in the chariot next to the king's chariot, and as he rode along, the people cried, "Bow the knee." And Pharaoh made him ruler over Egypt.

Pharaoh said that every man in Egypt should do as Joseph commanded him. Joseph went out over all the land and attended to saving up the corn for Pharaoh. In seven good years it grew well. When it was ripe and cut down, the people had much more than they could eat.

Then Joseph took a part of it and had it carried into those cities which were near the fields where it grew. He put it away in storehouses year by year that it might be kept safe until the seven years of famine should come. He saved up very much corn in this way. He finally stopped counting, for there was more of it than anyone could tell.

The seven good years were ended and the seven bad years began. The famine was not only in the land of Egypt; it was in other lands besides. In Egypt, however, there was bread, because Joseph had saved up the corn before the famine came. When the people had nothing to eat, they cried to Pharaoh for bread, and Pharaoh said, "Go to Joseph, and what he says to you, do."

Joseph opened all the storehouses where the corn was kept, and he sold it to the Egyptians. People came from other countries, also, to buy corn, because the famine was in the countries where they lived.

Joseph's Brothers Come to Egypt

NOW, JOSEPH'S BROTHERS were still living in the land of Canaan. It had been many years since they sold him to the Ishmaelites. They did not know what had become of him, but they thought he was dead. The famine was in Canaan, and they wanted food for their father and their little children to eat. They looked at one another as if they did not know where they should get it or what they should do.

Then Jacob said to them, "Why do you look one upon another? I have heard there is corn in Egypt. Go down there and buy some for us, that we may live and not die."

So Joseph's ten brothers left their home to go. But Benjamin, his youngest brother, stayed with his father in Canaan, for his father was afraid some evil might happen to him if he should go with them. So Joseph's brothers came down into Egypt with many other persons to buy corn, for the famine was in all the countries around Egypt.

Now, Joseph was governor over Egypt. It was he who sold corn to the people. His brothers came and bowed down before him with their faces to the earth. Joseph saw them and knew them, but he pretended he did not know them. He asked them, "From whence do you come?"

They answered, "From the land of Canaan, to buy food."

But though Joseph knew his brothers, they did not know him nor think at all that it was their brother whom they had sold to the Ishmaelites so many years before.

Joseph spoke roughly to them. "You are spies who are come into the land."

But his brothers answered, "No, my lord. We have come to buy food."

Yet Joseph seemed not to believe them, and he said again they were spies. But it was not because he was angry that he spoke roughly to them. He did so that they might not know him. He was soon going to be very kind to them, for Joseph was a good man and was willing to forgive his brothers their unkindness to him. Then they told Joseph that they were all brothers and that their father had twelve sons. One of them, they said, was with their father in the land of Canaan—that was Benjamin— and one, they said, "was not." They meant he was dead.

Yet Joseph still pretended not to believe them and said he would find out whether they spoke the truth or not, and this was the way he would do it: One of them should go home to Canaan to bring their youngest brother down to Egypt, but all the rest must stay till that one should come back. He put them in prison for three days. On the third day he spoke to them again, but this time he said that all but one might go home to take corn for their families to eat. They must leave one, however, so that Joseph might be sure the others would come back and bring their youngest brother with them.

When his brothers heard him say this and saw that he was in earnest and meant to do as he said, they were in great trouble. They did not know it was Joseph who spoke with them, yet they thought that God was punishing them for their sin in selling their brother to the Ishmaelites so long ago. They talked with each other about it and spoke of how wicked they had been.

Reuben, the one who had intended to take Joseph out of the pit and bring him back to his father, said to his brothers, "Did I not speak to you, saying, 'Do not sin against the child,' but you would not listen to me?"

Joseph heard them talking together, for they thought he could not understand what they said because he had talked with them only in the Egyptian language and had had an interpreter to explain what he said. Yet Joseph understood every word they spoke, and he had to go away from them that they might not see him, for what they said made him weep. Afterward he came back and talked to them again. Still he pretended to think they were spies. Then he took Simeon, one of his brothers, and bound him, for Simeon was to stay in Egypt while the others went home after Benjamin.

Joseph commanded his servants to fill his brothers' sacks with corn and to put the money that each one had paid back again into his sack; but he did not tell his brothers of this, and they did not know that their money was put back. So when their asses were loaded, all of them except Simeon started on their journey to their home in Canaan. They came to the inn on the road where travelers stopped to rest. As one of them opened his sack to give his ass some food out of it, he saw his money, for it was in the mouth of his sack. He said to his brothers, "My money is given back to me; it is in my sack." Then they were afraid, for they did not know who had put it there.

They continued on their journey and came to Jacob, their father, in the land of Canaan and told him of the things that had happened to them while they were gone.

They said, "The man who is the lord of the country spoke roughly to us and took us for spies. And we said, 'We are not spies.' So he said, 'This is how I shall know whether you are true men: Leave one of your brothers with me, take food to your families, and go and bring your youngest brother to me. Then I shall know that you are not spies but true men. I will give your brother up to you again, and you may buy corn in the land without interference thereafter.' "

When they came to empty corn out of their sacks, they found every man's bundle of money that he had paid for the corn put back into the sack. They and their father were afraid.

Jacob was troubled. He said to his sons that they had taken away his children from him; Joseph was gone, and Simeon was gone, and now they wanted to take Benjamin away.

Then Reuben, who had two sons of his own, spoke to his father, saying, "Slay my two sons if I do not bring Benjamin back to you. Give him to me and I will bring him to you again."

But Jacob said that Benjamin should not go down to Egypt. Joseph was dead, he said, and if any harm happened to Benjamin, it would be greater trouble than he could bear.

The famine was very dreadful in the land of Canaan. When they had eaten up the corn which they brought out of Egypt, Jacob said to his sons, "Go, buy us a little food."

Judah told his father they would go down and buy food if he would let Benjamin go with them, but if he would not let Benjamin go, they would not go down, for the man, the lord of the country, had said to them, "You shall not see my face unless your brother is with you." Then Israel —that was Jacob, for now he had two names—asked his sons why they were so unkind to him as to tell the man they had another brother at home.

But they answered, "The man asked us, saying, 'Is your father yet alive? Have you another brother?' Could we know that he would say, 'Bring your brother down'?"

Then their father, Israel, told them that if they must take Benjamin, they had better take also a present to the man.

"Do this," he said. "Take some of the best fruits and carry down the man a present—a little balm, and a little honey, spices and myrrh, nuts and almonds. Take more money with you, and also the money that was brought back in the mouths of your sacks; perhaps it was a mistake. Take also your brother, and arise and go again to the man." And Israel prayed for his sons, that God would make the man kind to them, for, he said, if his children were taken away from him, he would be left lonely and sorrowful indeed.

So they took the present and the money and Benjamin, and went down to Egypt and stood before Joseph again. And when Joseph saw Benjamin with them, he said to his steward who took care of his house, "Bring these men home and make ready, for they shall eat dinner with me at noon."

The servant did as Joseph commanded. The men were afraid when they came to Joseph's house. They said to one another that they were brought there because they had carried the money home in their sacks the first time, and that now Joseph was going to blame them for it, so that he might make them his slaves.

They came near to Joseph's steward, and talked with him at the door of the house, saying, "O sir, indeed we came down the first time only to buy food." They told him that when they stopped at the inn on the way home to Canaan, they opened their sacks and found the money they had paid for their corn put back into their sacks. And now, they said, they had brought that money back with them and other money, also, to buy food.

Then Joseph's steward told them not to fear. He brought Simeon out to them, the one who had been left bound in Egypt while they went home to Canaan. The steward gave them water to wash their feet, and he gave food to their asses. They made ready the present which they had brought for Joseph, to give it to him when he should come home at noon, for they had heard they were to stay and eat dinner there.

When Joseph came, they brought his present into the house and bowed themselves down before him to the earth. He spoke kindly to them, saying, "Is your father well, the old man of whom you spoke? Is he yet alive?"

They answered, "Your servant, our father, is in good health; he is yet alive." And they bowed down to him again.

Joseph looked and saw his brother Benjamin and said, "Is this your younger brother of whom you spoke to me?" And he said, "May God be good to you, my son."

Then Joseph made haste to find a place where he might go and weep. He went into his chamber and wept there, because he was so full of joy at seeing his brother. Afterward he washed his face and came out and kept back the tears, so that his brothers could not tell that he had been weeping.

He told his servants to set bread on the table, and they set bread for Joseph in one place, to eat by himself, and for his brothers in another place, to eat by themselves. This was because the Egyptians would not eat with the Hebrews—that is, with the sons of Jacob—and Joseph wanted to pretend that he was an Egyptian. When his brothers came to take their seats, they found that the oldest one had the first seat, and the next oldest the next seat, and so they were all placed according to their ages. Then they wondered who could have known how to place their seats in that way.

Joseph sent food to his brothers from his own table, and to Benjamin he sent five times as much as to any of the others, for he loved Benjamin more than the others. Joseph's brothers ate and drank with him in his house, but they did not know it was Joseph.

Joseph commanded the steward of his house to fill the men's sacks with food, as much as they could carry, and to put every man's money back in the mouth of his sack, as had been done when they came down into Egypt before. "And put my cup, the silver cup," he said, "in the sack of the youngest." The steward did as Joseph commanded.

In the morning, as soon as it was light, the men started on their journey back to Canaan. When they had gone out of the city, but were not far off, Joseph told his steward to follow after them and ask why they had taken his silver cup. So the steward followed after them. When he came up to them, he asked as Joseph had told him.

The men were very much surprised and wondered why the steward spoke such words to them. God forbid, they said, that they should do such a thing as steal Joseph's cup. They had brought back money which they found in their sacks when they went home to Canaan the first time; they could have kept it had they chosen to do so, but they brought it back of their own accord. If they had done this, they asked, would they now take from Joseph's house silver or gold which did not belong to them?

Then they told the steward that if any of them had taken the cup, he might put that one to death, and all the rest would be his servants. The steward answered that the one who had taken the cup should be his servant, but the rest should not be blamed. Then each of them quickly took down his sack from the back of the ass and rested it on the ground; then each opened his sack so that the steward could look into it. He looked, beginning with the sack of the oldest, leaving off with the sack of

the youngest, and he found the cup in Benjamin's sack.
Then they rent their clothes and loaded their asses and returned with him to the city.

They came to Joseph's house, for he was still there, and
they fell down before him on the ground. Joseph pretended to think they had really stolen his cup, and he
asked if they did not know he would find it out.

Then Judah spoke to him, saying, "What shall we say
to my lord? Or what shall we do that we may not be
punished? God has found out our wickedness. We are
all my lord's servants." But Joseph answered that only the
one who had the cup should be his servant; as for the rest,
they might go home to their father.

Judah came near to Joseph and begged him not to be
angry but to let him speak. Judah said that when they
came down to Egypt the first time Joseph asked them, saying, "Have you a father and a brother at home in the
country where you live?" And they told him they had a
father, an old man, and also a brother who was a
child yet, and that their father loved the boy, for his
mother was dead and his brother was dead. Joseph told
them to bring that younger brother down to Egypt that
he might see him. Then they had answered that the boy
could not leave his father, for, if he should do so, his father
would die. But Joseph told them that if they did not
bring their brother down, they should never see his face
again. So when they went home to their father, they told
him what Joseph had said. And after a while their father
wanted them to go down to Egypt again to buy a little
more food. But they said to him, "We cannot go unless our
youngest brother goes with us." Then their father told
them that if they took Benjamin and any harm should
happen to him while they were gone, he would die with
sorrow.

Judah said that if he went home without Benjamin,
their father would die. Judah had promised to bring him

back safely to his father and had told his father that if he did not bring him back he would bear the blame forever. Judah begged Joseph to let him stay and be his servant in Benjamin's place, and to let Benjamin go home to his father.

Joseph could hide himself from them no longer, and he commanded all his servants to go out of the room, so that no one was left but Joseph and his brothers. He then wept out loud, and his brothers heard him and saw him weeping. He said to them, "I am Joseph. Does my father yet live?" But they were afraid and could not answer him. Then Joseph said to them, "Come near to me, I pray you." When they came near, he said, "I am Joseph, your brother, whom you sold into Egypt."

He told them not to be troubled nor angry with themselves because they had sold him, for God had sent him into Egypt to save people by keeping them from starving in the famine. Joseph did not mean to say that his brothers did right when they sold him, but that God had made good come out of the evil which they had done. Joseph told them this so that they might not be unhappy and afraid. He loved them and had forgiven their unkindness to him. He did not want them to be unhappy now when he was so glad to see them once more.

Joseph told them that the famine had been in Egypt for two years, and it would be there five years longer. In these years there would be no harvest or planting of seed in the ground, for God had said the famine should last that long. Joseph told his brothers that God had sent him into Egypt before them to save them from starving.

He said to them, "Make haste and go back to my father in Canaan and say to him, 'Thus says your son Joseph: God has made me ruler over all Egypt. Come down to me, and you shall live in the best part of the land and shall be near to me; you and your children, your flocks and your herds, and all that you have.

" 'And I will take care of you, lest you and your family should come to be poor.' "

Joseph said to his brothers, "Your eyes see, and my brother Benjamin's eyes see, that it is my mouth that speaks to you. You shall tell my father of all my greatness in Egypt and of all that you have seen, and you shall make haste and bring my father here." Joseph leaned on his brother Benjamin's neck and wept, for he was more glad to see him than he could tell. Benjamin wept on Joseph's neck, too. And Joseph kissed all his brothers and wept on them. Afterward they talked with him.

When Pharaoh heard that Joseph's brothers had come, it pleased him well. He told Joseph to tell them they should load their beasts and go back to the land of Canaan and get their father, their wives, and their little children and bring them to him. They need bring nothing else, Pharaoh said, for it was the same as if all the good things in the land of Egypt belonged to them.

Joseph's brothers did so. Joseph gave them wagons for their wives and children to ride in, as Pharaoh had commanded, food to eat while they were gone, and raiment. To Benjamin he gave more than to any of the others, and also three hundred pieces of silver. To his father he sent twenty asses loaded with bread and meat and good things. Then he sent his brothers on their way.

The brothers went up out of Egypt and came to their father in Canaan. They said to him, "Joseph is yet alive. He is governor over all the land of Egypt."

It seemed too wonderful to be true, and Jacob did not believe them. Yet when he heard all the kind words that Joseph had spoken and saw the wagons which Pharaoh had sent to carry him, Jacob believed what his sons told him. He said, "It is enough. Joseph, my son, is yet alive. I will go and see him before I die."

So Jacob and his sons and their families and servants went down into Egypt to live.

The Child Moses

AFTER MANY YEARS the Pharaoh who had been kind to the people of Israel died and another Pharaoh took his place. By this time there were a great many Israelites in the country of Egypt. The new Pharaoh was afraid that they might rise up and try to take his kingdom from him, so he treated them cruelly. He made them work very hard and he ordered that all the boy babies should be put to death.

There was a man among the Israelites named Amram. His wife's name was Jochebed, and God gave them a son. The child was very beautiful, and his mother loved him. She feared that some of Pharaoh's servants would come and take him from her in order to kill him. Therefore, she hid him for three months after he was born, but then found she could hide him no longer. So she took a little ark, or boat, made out of the long weeds that grew by the river, and daubed it over with pitch to keep out the water. And she put her baby into the ark and laid it carefully among the rushes at the edge of the river.

The little baby's sister waited, not far off, to see what might happen to him.

Soon the daughter of the Pharaoh came down to bathe in the river, and she and her maidens walked along by the river's side. When she saw the ark among the rushes, she sent one of them to bring it. The maiden brought the snug little ark, and as Pharaoh's daughter looked into it, the little boy wept. She pitied him and said, "This is one of the Hebrews' children."

Then the baby's sister, who had been watching, came near and spoke to the king's daughter, saying, "May I not go and call one of the Hebrew women to come and nurse the child for you?"

She said, "Go."

So the baby's sister went to her own home and called her mother.

When she came, Pharaoh's daughter said to her, "Take this child away and nurse it for me, and I will give you your wages." So his mother carried him back to her own home and nursed him there.

After a while Pharaoh's daughter sent for the child. When his mother brought him to her, Pharaoh's daughter took him into her house to be as her own son. She called his name Moses, which means, "drawn out," because, she said, "I drew him out of the water."

Moses grew up in the palace and was given the same training as the Egyptian boys in the palace. Yet when he grew to be a man he knew that he was not an Egyptian, but an Israelite.

So he went to live with his own people.

Moses
Becomes a Leader

MANY THINGS HAPPENED to Moses during his lifetime, but there was one day he never forgot.

He was on a place called Mount Horeb and God spoke to him out of a burning bush, saying, "Moses, Moses."

Moses answered, "Here am I."

God told him not to come near, but to take his shoes from off his feet, because the place where he stood was holy ground. It was holy, and Moses was not to come near, because God was there. God said to him, also, "I am the God of thy father, the God of Abraham, the God of Isaac, and the God of Jacob."

Moses hid his face, for he was afraid to look upon God. Then God told him that He had seen the affliction of the children of Israel, and had heard their cries, and had come down to set them free from the Egyptians.

The Lord told Moses that He would send him to Pharaoh so that he might tell Pharaoh to let the children of Israel go. The Lord said that Moses should lead them out of Egypt and should bring them to that mountain where He was then talking with him.

Moses was afraid to go. He said, "Who am I that I should go to Pharaoh and bring the children of Israel out of Egypt?"

God said to him, "Certainly I will be with thee to help thee."

God commanded Moses to go and tell the children of Israel that the Lord God of their fathers had sent him to bring them out of Egypt to a good land where they should have milk to drink and honey to eat. After Moses had told them this, he was to speak to Pharaoh and ask him to let the people go. But Moses said to the Lord that when he should come into Egypt and tell the children of Israel these things, he was sure they would not listen to him, nor believe that the Lord had spoken to him at all.

Now, Moses held a rod in his hand, and the Lord said to him, "What is that in thy hand?"

Moses answered, "A rod."

The Lord said, "Cast it on the ground."

Moses cast it on the ground, and God made it change into a serpent. Moses was afraid of it and fled away before it.

Then the Lord said, "Put out thy hand and take it by the tail."

Moses took it and it changed back again into a rod in his hand.

Then the Lord said to Moses, "Put now thy hand into thy bosom." Moses put his hand into his bosom, and when he took it out it was white as snow, for it was covered with a dreadful disease called leprosy, which made it look white like snow. And God said, "Put thy hand into thy bosom again." And Moses put it into his bosom, and when he took it out it was well and covered with leprosy no more.

God gave Moses power to do these two wonderful works, or miracles, so that when the children of Israel should see them, they might believe that God had sent him. But if they would not believe after he had done both, then God said Moses should take some water out of the river that was in Egypt and pour it on the dry ground; the water would be changed into blood on the ground where Moses had poured it. But Moses still did not want to go, and he began to make excuses for not going. He said he could not speak well before the people. But the Lord commanded him again to go and said He would teach him what to say. Yet Moses begged the Lord to send someone else. Then the Lord was angry because Moses was still unwilling to go.

Moses had a brother named Aaron. God said that Aaron could speak well, and that he should go with Moses into Egypt. Moses would tell Aaron what to say, but Aaron would tell it to the people; God said He would teach them both what they should do. He told Moses to take his rod in his hand, for with it he should do wonderful things.

When God had finished talking with him, Moses went to the home of Jethro, in the land of Midian. Jethro had befriended Moses and had cared for him for many years. Moses asked Jethro for permission to go back into Egypt that he might see his brethren, the children of Israel. Jethro gave him permission to go.

The Lord commanded Aaron, Moses' brother, to come out and meet him at Mount Horeb. Aaron came there and met Moses, and he was glad and kissed him. And Moses told Aaron of all the words that God had spoken. Then Moses and Aaron went into Egypt and spoke to the children of Israel. They could not speak to all of them at once, because there were too many to hear, so they sent for the chief men among them, called elders, and told them, and the elders told the people. They showed them the miracles, also, that God had given Moses power to do. When the children of Israel saw these, they believed that God had sent Moses and Aaron, and that Moses was coming, as he had promised, to take them out of Egypt.

The Plagues of Egypt

Aftᴇʀ ᴛʜᴇʏ had spoken with the elders, Moses and Aaron went to Pharaoh and said, "Thus says the Lord God of Israel: 'Let My people go that they may hold a feast unto Me in the wilderness.'"

Pharaoh answered, "Who is the Lord that I should obey Him? I know not the Lord; neither will I let the children of Israel go."

Moses and Aaron told him that it was God who had spoken to them. They begged Pharaoh to let them go, lest, if they should not, God might punish them for their disobedience. Pharaoh asked Moses and Aaron why they kept people from their work, telling them they were to go out of Egypt. He told Moses and Aaron to go and work themselves.

Pharaoh was very angry and made the children of Israel

work much harder than before.

The Lord told Moses to go again to Pharaoh and demand that he let the children of Israel leave Egypt.

Moses went to Pharaoh and did as the Lord commanded. Again Pharaoh refused. Then Moses performed many miracles. He turned his rod into a serpent and the river into blood.

The Lord sent plagues down upon Egypt. Frogs came up from the rivers and entered the homes and the palace. Still Pharaoh would not let the people go. Then the Lord sent a plague of flies, a sickness that killed the cattle, a great storm of hail, a swarm of locusts that ate all growing stuff, and a great darkness that lasted three days and nights. Each time Pharaoh promised that if Moses would take away the plague, he would let the people go. But each time when the plague was taken away, Pharaoh refused to let the Israelites leave the country.

Moses told Pharaoh of one more punishment. The Lord would come, Moses said, about the middle of the night, and He would cause the oldest son in every house to die. Pharaoh's oldest son and the oldest sons of all his servants would die on that dreadful night, and there would be a great cry of trouble and grief over all the land such as had never been before and would never be again. But none of the sons of the children of Israel should die, so that Pharaoh might know that he and his people were the ones whom the Lord intended to punish. After this punishment, Moses said, the Egyptians would bow down to him and beg him to take the people and go out of the land.

When Moses had told Pharaoh this, Pharaoh went from him in great anger.

The Lord told Moses and Aaron that every man among the children of Israel should take a lamb from the flock, and keep it four days and then kill it. Then he was to take a bunch of a plant called hyssop, dip it in the blood of the lamb, and go to the door of his house and strike the hyssop

73

upon each side of the door and over it, so that there would be three marks of blood outside of every house where the children of Israel lived. When the man had done this, he was to go into the house again, and no one was to come out of it until morning.

The lamb which had been killed was to be roasted with fire, and every person in the house was to eat of it that night. This is the way they were to eat of it: with their clothes girded around them, their shoes on their feet, and their staves in their hands, all ready to go out of Egypt. They were to make haste while they ate of it, because the Lord would go through the land that night and would cause the oldest sons of all the Egyptians to die, so that Pharaoh and his people should let the children of Israel go. But the Lord promised that when He saw the marks of the blood on the houses where the children of Israel lived, He would pass over those houses and not harm anyone in them. Therefore, the supper of the lamb, which the children of Israel ate that night, was called the Lord's Passover. And the Lord commanded them, at this supper and for seven days afterward, to eat only one kind of bread. It was called unleavened bread, because there was no leaven, or yeast, used in making it.

Moses called the elders of the children of Israel to him and told them what the Lord had said, and the elders told the people. Then every man took his lamb and kept it four days. Afterward he killed it, dipped the bunch of hyssop in its blood, and struck the wood outside of his door, so that there were three marks of blood on every house where the children of Israel lived.

Those who were in the house ate of the lamb that night; they ate of it with their clothes girded around them, with their shoes on their feet, and with their staves in their hands, all ready to go out of Egypt.

The same night, in the middle of the night, the Lord passed through the land. Wherever He saw the marks of blood on a house, He passed over the house and did no harm to anyone in it. On the houses of the Egyptians there were no marks of blood, and the Lord sent His destroying angel into every Egyptian's house and caused the oldest son there to die. Pharaoh's son and the sons of his servants died. And the king rose up in the night, as did all his people, and there was a great cry of distress through all the land, for there was not a house where there was not one dead.

The Pharaoh called for Moses and Aaron and told them to go out of Egypt and to take all the children of Israel with them. He said, "Take your flocks and your herds, and be gone."

The Egyptians begged them to go quickly, for they were afraid that the Lord would cause all the Egyptians to die.

The children of Israel went, carrying their clothes bound up with their kneading troughs on their shoulders. The Egyptians gave them jewels of silver, jewels of gold, and raiment, also, so they went out with great riches. Many other persons who were not Israelites went with them.

Out of Bondage

WHEN PHARAOH HAD let the children of Israel go, the Lord led them toward Canaan. The route was not the shortest way, which passed through the land of the Philistines, lest the Philistines should make war against them and they should be discouraged and go back to Egypt. The Lord showed them another way, toward the Red Sea.

The people journeyed to a place called Etham on the edge of the wilderness. There they set up their tents and made a camp. As they journeyed, the Lord went before them in a cloud to show them the way. The cloud was shaped like a pillar reaching up toward heaven. They could see it all the time. In the day it was the color of a cloud, but at night it was the color of fire. It gave them light at night, so that they could journey both in the day and in the night when the Lord commanded. And the Lord did not take away the pillar of cloud in the day or the pillar of fire in the night from before the people.

After the children of Israel had left Egypt, Pharaoh and his servants were sorry that they had let them go. "Why have we let Israel go from serving us?" they said.

Then the Pharaoh made ready his chariot and took with him all the chariots in which his soldiers rode out to battle and went after them. He came up to them while they were encamping by the sea. When Pharaoh came near, the children of Israel looked back and saw the Egyptians marching after them. They were greatly afraid and cried out loudly to the Lord.

They blamed Moses for bringing them away from Egypt. It would have been better for them, they said, to stay and work for the Egyptians than to be slain there in the wilderness. But Moses told the people not to fear.

He said to them, "Wait and see how the Lord will save you, for the Egyptians, whom you have seen today, you shall see no more forever. The Lord will fight for you, and you need do nothing but be still."

Pharaoh and his army followed after the children of Israel until they had almost reached them. Then the cloud which went before the children of Israel changed its place and came behind them. It came between the children of Israel and Pharaoh's army. That side of it which was turned toward Pharaoh's army grew very dark, and his soldiers could not see to come any nearer to the children of Israel all that night. The other side of the cloud, which was turned toward the children of Israel, was bright like fire and gave them light in their camp.

The Lord said to Moses, "Speak unto the children of Israel, that they go forward. And lift up thy rod and stretch out thy hand over the sea, and the children of Israel shall go on dry ground through the sea."

Moses lifted up his rod and stretched out his hand over the sea. The Lord sent a great wind all that night, which blew the water away from that part of the sea, so that the bottom of the sea was left dry. The children of Israel went down into it and walked on the bottom of the sea on dry ground. The waters were piled up high on each side of them like a wall, yet the waters did not come down to drown them all the while they were walking through the sea.

That is the way the children of Israel went out of Egypt. They walked through the Red Sea on dry ground until they all came safe to the other side.

When Pharaoh saw that they had gone, he and his chariots and his horsemen followed after them, for he thought that they would be able to pass through the sea as the children of Israel had done. In the morning the Lord looked on the Egyptians as they were marching through the sea. He made the wheels of their chariots come off, so that they had to drive very slowly, and He troubled the Egyptians. They were afraid and said to each other, "Let us make haste back, for the Lord fights against us, and He fights for the children of Israel."

Before they had time to go, the Lord told Moses to stretch out his hand over the sea once more. Moses stretched out his hand, and the waters came together again and covered the Egyptians in the bottom of the sea. Then all Pharaoh's horses and his horsemen and all his army were drowned. Not one of them was left alive.

Moses and the Israelites were safe on the other side of the Red Sea. There they sang a song of praise to the Lord for saving them from Pharaoh.

The Ten Commandments

FOR MANY, MANY days Moses and the children of Israel journeyed through the wilderness. The people became very hungry, for nothing grew on the desert. They were angry with Moses for bringing them to such a barren place.

Moses called upon the Lord and told Him of the anger of the people. And God spoke to him and promised that He would send food to the Israelites.

The Lord did as He had promised. He sent quail so that the people might have meat. In the morning the ground was covered with something white, like frost. Moses said, "This is the food the Lord has sent." The people tasted it and found that it was good. Every night the Lord sent the food and every morning the people gathered enough for that one day. And they called this new food manna.

At another time the people called upon Moses and said they had no water for their children or for their beasts.

"Give us water that we may drink," they commanded him.

Moses again asked the Lord what he should do. And the Lord told Moses to go to a certain stone and hit it with his staff, and water would gush forth. Moses obeyed the Lord. He took his rod in his hand and struck the rock, and water came out from it.

In the third month after the children of Israel went out of Egypt, they came near the mountain called Sinai and encamped before it. Moses went up on the mountain, and the Lord spoke to him. He told him to tell the people that they had seen how He punished the Egyptians for their sakes and afterward brought the children of Israel out of that land. And now, the Lord said, if they would obey His commandments, He would love them more than any other people.

The Lord said He would come down in a thick cloud and speak with Moses on Mount Sinai, so that the people should hear Him. He commanded Moses to tell them to wash their clothes and make themselves clean, and to be very careful not to sin, and to be ready for the third day.

On that day, God said, none of them might go on the mountain, for whoever should go there would surely be put to death. But when they should hear the great sound of a trumpet, they should come and stand at the foot of the mountain.

After the Lord had spoken these things, Moses went down and told the people. They washed their clothes and were careful not to sin. And on the third day there were thundering and lightning and a thick cloud on the mount. A trumpet sounded very loudly, and all the people trembled when they heard it. Then Moses led them out of the camp, and they came and stood near the foot of the mount. All the mountain smoked because the Lord came down in fire upon it, and the mountain shook greatly. Moses spoke, and God answered him and called him to the top of the mount.

And God spoke, on Mount Sinai, these words of the Ten Commandments:

"THOU SHALT HAVE NO OTHER GODS BEFORE ME.

"THOU SHALT NOT MAKE ANY GRAVEN IMAGE, NOR BOW DOWN TO IT, NOR WORSHIP IT.

"THOU SHALT NOT TAKE THE NAME OF THE LORD THY GOD IN VAIN.

"REMEMBER THE SABBATH DAY, TO KEEP IT HOLY.

"HONOR THY FATHER AND THY MOTHER.

"THOU SHALT NOT KILL.

"THOU SHALT NOT COMMIT ADULTERY.

"THOU SHALT NOT STEAL.

"THOU SHALT NOT BEAR FALSE WITNESS AGAINST THY NEIGHBOR.

"THOU SHALT NOT COVET ANYTHING THAT IS THY NEIGHBOR'S."

So the Lord gave Moses the Ten Commandments by which the people should be governed.

All the people heard the thunderings and the sound of the trumpet. They saw the lightning and the mountain smoking. They heard God's voice and were afraid. Then they said to Moses, "Speak with us and we will hear, but let not God speak with us, lest we die." But Moses told them that God had not come to cause them to die, but to make them fear to sin against Him. The people stood a little ways off from the mountain, but Moses went up on the mountain near to the dark cloud where God was.

There God talked with him and gave him many more laws for the children of Israel to obey. Afterward Moses came down from the mount. He wrote those laws in a book and read them to the people. When the people heard them, they promised to obey all the words that the Lord had spoken.

Ever since, men have remembered the Ten Commandments and tried to keep them.

Gideon

AFTER THE ISRAELITES had arrived in the land which the Lord had promised them and had conquered it, they lived peaceably for many years. Then the Midianites came down from the hills and treated them cruelly. They drove the people from their homes. They destroyed their grain and cattle. The children of Israel cried to the Lord to help them.

There was a man of the children of Israel named Gideon who was threshing wheat one day in order that he might hide it from the Midianites. The Lord came, in the form of an angel, and spoke kindly to him. Gideon told the Lord of the troubles that had come to the children of Israel because of the Midianites.

The Lord said to him, "Thou shalt set the children of Israel free from the Midianites."

Gideon answered, "O my Lord, how shall I set Israel free?"

The Lord said, "Surely I will be with thee. Thou shalt destroy their whole army, as if it were but one man."

Then Gideon said to the Lord, "Stay, I pray Thee, until I can go and bring Thee an offering."

And the Lord answered, "I will stay till thou comest again."

Then Gideon went and killed a kid and made it ready. He put the meat into a basket and brought it out to the Lord. The Lord told him to lay it upon a rock that was there, and Gideon did so. Then the Lord reached forth the end of the staff that was in His hand and touched the flesh. There rose up fire out of the rock and burnt up the offering. And the Lord went away from Gideon's sight.

The army of the Midianites came and made their camp in the valley of Jezreel. Then Gideon blew a trumpet and called the children of Israel to go with him and fight against them. He sent messengers through different parts of the land, and many of the people came.

Gideon asked the Lord to do a miracle for him, that he might know the Lord would certainly help him when he fought against the Midianites. Gideon said he would take a fleece of wool and leave it out on the ground all night. If in the morning it should have dew on it, and the ground all around it be dry, then he should know that the Lord would surely help him to set the children of Israel free. And Gideon took the fleece of wool and left it on the ground all night, as he had said. He rose early in the morning and went to it and found it full of dew. He wrung dew out of it with his hands and filled a bowl with water. The ground all around it was dry.

Gideon spoke to the Lord again. He prayed that the Lord would not be angry if he asked Him to do one thing more. Then he said he would put the fleece out another night. He asked that this time it might be dry, but the ground all around it wet with dew. He left the fleece of wool out another night, and in the morning, when he looked, it was dry. No dew was on it, but the ground all around it was wet with dew. So Gideon knew by these miracles which the Lord had done for him that the Lord would certainly help him when he should go out to fight against the Midianites.

Then Gideon and all the army of Israel rose up early and came near the camp of the Midianites. The Lord spoke to Gideon, saying there were too many men in the army of Israel. If such great numbers of them should go to the battle and gain the victory, they would say they had gained it by their own strength, and not that the Lord had gained it for them. The Lord ordered Gideon to tell the men in his army that all who felt afraid might go back to their homes. When Gideon told them this, twenty-two thousand went from the camp of Israel. There were left ten thousand men.

The Lord spoke to Gideon again, saying, "There are yet too many. Bring them down to the water, and I will show thee which of them shall go with thee to the battle."

So Gideon brought them to the water. All the men were thirsty and began to drink. But they drank in different ways—some lifting the water in their hands to their mouths, and some stooping down and putting their mouths into the water. The Lord commanded Gideon to put those who drank out of their hands apart by themselves. When he had done so, there were three hundred of them. It was the Lord who made them drink in this way, so that they might be separated from the others. Only these three hundred men should go with him to the battle, the Lord told Gideon.

The same night the Lord commanded Gideon to arise and go with his three hundred men against the Midianites, for, He said, He would give him victory. If Gideon were

afraid to go with so few, then the Lord told him to go near their camp first with his servant, not to fight against them, but in the dark where they could not see him, to listen and hear what they said. The Lord promised that after Gideon had done this, he would feel no more fear, but should be willing to go and fight against them.

Now, the Midianites lay along in the valley like grass-hoppers—there were so many of them—and their camels no one could number. Gideon went down with his servant in the night and came near to their camp and heard two of them talking together. One was telling the other of a dream he had dreamed. He said, "I saw in my dream a loaf of barley bread come tumbling into our camp. It struck against a tent and threw it down, so that the tent lay flat upon the ground."

The man who heard him answered, saying, "That loaf of bread means the sword of Gideon, for the Lord is going to give all our host into his hand."

When Gideon heard this, he went back to the three hundred men and told them to rise up and come, for the Lord would give them the victory. He set them in three different companies and put in every man's hand a trumpet and a pitcher, with a lighted lamp inside the pitcher. He told them that when they came near to the camp of the Midianites, they must look at him and do as he did. When he should blow with his trumpet, they must all blow and cry out, "The sword of the Lord and of Gideon."

So he came with the three hundred men near to the camp of the Midianites in the middle of the night. Suddenly they all blew with their trumpets, broke the pitchers that were in their hands, and cried aloud, "The sword of the Lord and of Gideon."

When the Midianites heard the noise and saw the burning lamps that had been hidden in the pitchers, they cried out with fear and fled. The Lord made them afraid of the men of Israel and afraid of each other, also, so that they fought among themselves in their confusion.

Gideon followed them to the River Jordan. He passed over the river after the two kings of the Midianites, who fled before him with fifteen thousand men—all that were left of their great army. Gideon and his three hundred men overtook them and took the two kings captives. So the Midianites were driven out of Canaan, and the children of Israel had to serve them no longer.

Samson

THE CHILDREN OF Israel sinned and displeased the Lord, and the Philistines waged war against them and made them their servants for forty years.

There was at that time a man of Israel named Manoah. Both he and his wife loved the Lord. They had no children. The angel of the Lord spoke to the woman and told her they would have a son and that he should be a Nazarite to God. This meant that he would be set apart, to serve God. He was never to drink wine, and his parents were to let his hair grow without ever cutting it. Persons who were Nazarites drank no wine nor cut their hair as others did, for so the Lord commanded them. The angel of the Lord said, also, that Manoah's son would be the one who would begin to set the children of Israel free.

God gave Manoah and his wife the son he had

promised them. They called him Samson. The child grew and the Lord was kind to him and blessed him and gave him great strength.

One day Samson passed through some vineyards in a lonely part of the country. A young lion met him and roared at him. The Lord gave Samson strength to kill the lion as easily as if it had been a kid. He did this with his hands alone, for he had no sword or spear. Sometime later when he passed the place where he had killed the lion, he turned aside to look at its dead body. A swarm of bees had made honey there. He took some of the honey in his hands and ate of it. Afterward he gave some to his father and mother, but he did not tell them that he had taken it out of the dead body of the lion.

Soon after this he made a feast for his friends. It lasted seven days and thirty of the Philistines came to it. Samson told them he would give them a riddle so that they might find out what it meant and tell him. If they should do so before the seven days of the feast were ended, he promised to give them thirty suits of raiment. But if they could not find out his riddle, they were to give him thirty suits. The Philistines agreed and asked for his riddle.

These were the words of the riddle: Out of the eater came forth meat, and out of the strong came forth sweetness. It meant: Out of the strong lion that was ready to eat Samson, Samson had taken sweet honey for himself to eat. But he did not tell the Philistines what it meant. They tried for three days to find out for themselves, but could not. They were very angry. On the seventh day they came to his wife, who was also a Philistine, and told her that they would burn her and her father's house unless she helped them to find out the meaning of the riddle.

So she begged her husband to tell her, weeping before him and saying that he did not love her because he had given the riddle to her friends, yet had not told her what it meant.

But Samson answered, "I have not told my father or my mother. Shall I tell you?"

She continued to weep before him all the time that was left of the feast. At last he told her because she troubled him. When he had told her, she told the Philistines. They came to Samson on the seventh day, just before the end of the feast, and pretended they had themselves found out his riddle.

They said, "What is sweeter than honey, and what is stronger than a lion?" Samson knew that his wife had told them.

After this Samson went home to his father's house.

At the time of wheat harvest Samson went to Timnath to visit his wife and to bring her a kid. But when he came to her house, her father forbade him to go in. Samson was very angry. He went out and caught three hundred foxes, tied firebrands, or pieces of blazing wood, to their tails, and let them loose in the fields and vineyards of the Philistines. They set fire to the grain, and it was burned up, both that which had been cut and piled in shocks, and that which was still growing in the field. The grapevines and olive trees were burned, also.

The Philistines said, "Who has done this?" When they learned that it was Samson, they took his wife and her father as prisoners. Samson fought against the Philistines and slew many of them. Afterward he went to the top of a rock called Etam and stayed there.

The Philistines came up to take him, and they made their camp in the land of Israel. The men of Israel said to them, "Why are you come up against us?"

They answered, "To bind Samson, that we may do to him as he has done to us."

Three thousand men of the children of Israel went to the top of the rock Etam, where Samson was, and said to him, "Do you not know that the Philistines are rulers over us? Why have you done these things?"

Samson answered, "Because they have done evil to me, I have done evil to them." Then the men of Israel told him they had come to bind him in order that they might give him to the Philistines. Samson asked whether they would promise not to put him to death, if he should let them bind him. They answered, "We will not put you to death, but will bind you fast and give you to the Philistines."

Samson let them bind him with two new cords, and they took him to the Philistines' camp. As he came near to it, the Philistines saw him and were glad. They shouted against him. But the Lord gave Samson such strength that he broke the cords off from him as easily as if they had been burned by fire. He found the jawbone of an ass and took it in his hand. With it he fought against the Philistines and slew a thousand men. He said, "With the jawbone of an ass, heaps upon heaps, with the jaw of an ass have I slain a thousand men." Then he threw away the bone that he had used as a weapon.

He came to a city called Gaza and went into a house there. The Philistines lived in Gaza, and when they heard that Samson had come, they shut the gates of the city and watched by them all night so that they could capture him when he left. They said, "In the morning we shall kill him." But in the middle of the night, Samson rose up and came to the gates. When he found them shut, he dragged up the two posts to which the gates were fastened. He took the posts and the two great gates and the bar which went across them on the inside to keep them shut, and put them all upon his shoulders and carried them a good way off to the top of a hill.

We have read that Samson was a Nazarite, and that persons who were Nazarites were commanded not to cut their hair. Samson's hair had never been cut and had grown thick and long.

There was in that land a woman named Delilah, and

Samson used to go to her house. When the lords of the Philistines knew of it, they came to her and promised to give her eleven hundred pieces of silver if she would find out for them how they might bind Samson and make him their captive so that they could do with him as they pleased. Therefore, when Samson came to Delilah's house, she begged him to tell her what made him so strong and how he might be bound so that he would not be able to break loose again.

Samson told her that if he were bound with seven green withes—that is, cords made out of twigs or thin branches of trees twisted together—he would not be able to break them. When Delilah told the lords of the Philistines, they brought her seven green withes, and Samson let her bind him with them. She had men hidden in the room to take him if he could not break them. When she had bound him, she cried out, "The Philistines are coming to take you, Samson." She did this to discover whether or not he could break the green withes. As soon as she had spoken these words, he broke them as easily as if they were so many threads.

Delilah said to him that he had mocked her and told her lies. She begged him again to tell her how he might be bound. Samson answered that if he were bound with two new ropes which had never been used he would not be able to break loose. So she took two new ropes and bound him, having men hidden in the room this time, also. After she had bound him, she cried as before that the Philistines were coming to take him. Samson broke the new ropes from off his arms as easily as he had broken the green withes.

Delilah told him again that he had spoken lies to her. She begged him once more to tell her how he might be bound. Samson said that if she would plait, or weave, his long hair in a certain way, his great strength would go from him so that they could do with him as they chose.

When she had plaited his hair and fastened it as he told her, she cried out again that the Philistines were coming to take him. But when he heard these words, he rose up and went away, as strong as before.

Then she said to him, "How can you say, 'I love you,' when you have mocked me these three times?" She begged him every day to tell her; she would let him have no rest. She troubled him with her words until at last he told her the truth. He said that he had been a Nazarite ever since he was born, that his hair had never been cut, and that if it were shaven off from his head, he would be strong no longer, but as weak as other men.

Delilah saw that he had not deceived her. She sent word to the lords of the Philistines, saying, "Come but once more, for this time he has told me the truth." They came to her and brought the money they had promised. Then, while Samson was asleep, she called a man to shave the hair from his head. After it was done, she cried out that the Philistines were coming to take him.

He woke from his sleep and said he would go out against them as he used to do when she spoke these words to him before. He did not know that the Lord had taken his great strength from him. But the Philistines took him easily, for he could no longer fight against them. They bound him with chains made of brass. They put out his eyes and shut him up in prison, where they made him work very hard turning a millstone to grind their corn.

Now, while he was shut up in prison his hair grew, and the Lord gave him strength again. But the Philistines did not know this.

The lords of the Philistines called the people together in their idol's house to offer up a sacrifice to their idol, whose name was Dagon, and to rejoice because Samson was taken. The people came and praised their idol. They said it was he who helped them to take Samson and make him their captive. They were all pleased and merry. Then they said, "Send for Samson, that he may make sport for us."

So they sent for him and brought poor, blind Samson out of the prison. They made sport of him and set him between two pillars in the house of their idol.

The house was full of men and women, and all the lords of the Philistines were there. There were also great numbers of people on the roof. They looked down to see those who were in the house mocking Samson and making sport of him. A boy held him by the hand to lead him because he could not see. Samson asked the boy to let him feel the pillars which held up the house so that he might lean against them. When he stood between them, he put out his hands and touched the pillars.

Then Samson prayed, saying, "O Lord, remember me, I pray Thee, and give me strength only this once."

He put his arms around the pillars, one around one pillar and the other around the other pillar, and he said, "Let me die with the Philistines." He bent down and pulled the pillars together with all his might until they were moved from their places. The house fell upon the lords of the Philistines and upon all the people, killing great numbers of them.

Samson died with them.

Ruth

I~N THE DAYS~ when the judges ruled over Israel, there was a famine in Canaan. A man of the children of Israel, who lived in the city of Bethlehem, went to stay for a while in the land of Moab. His wife and their two sons went with him. The man's name was Elimelech. His wife's name was Naomi. After they had come into Moab, the man died, but his sons took wives of the women of Moab and lived for about ten years. Then they died, also. Their mother, Naomi, was left alone with her two daughters-in-law.

Naomi heard that the famine was over in Canaan and that the Lord had given the people food again. She rose up to leave the land of Moab and go back to Canaan, to the city of Bethlehem.

She asked her daughters-in-law if they would not rather

stay in Moab, which was their own land, where they were born and where their relatives lived.

When her daughters-in-law heard what she said, they were troubled and wept. One of them, named Orpah, kissed Naomi and bade her farewell and went away to her own home. But the other, whose name was Ruth, would not leave her.

Ruth told Naomi not to ask her to leave.

Ruth said, "Where you go, I will go, and where you live, I will live; your friends shall be my friends, and your God, my God; where you die, I will die, and there will I be buried." Ruth asked the Lord to punish her if she ever left Naomi, as long as they both should live.

So the two traveled until they came into Canaan, to the city of Bethlehem, where Naomi used to live. The people remembered her. All of them spoke about her coming back to the city. "Is this Naomi?" they asked.

Naomi was very sorrowful and answered, "Call me not Naomi, which means *pleasant;* but call me Mara, which means *bitter,* because the Lord has dealt very bitterly with me." She meant that the Lord had sent her great trouble. When she went away from Bethlehem, so many years before, her husband and her two sons had been with her. Now, when she came back, they were all dead.

It was in the beginning of the barley harvest, while the people of Canaan were cutting their grain, that Ruth and Naomi came to Bethlehem.

Ruth said to Naomi, "Let me go now out to the field and glean ears of corn."

To glean in the field was to pick up the grain that the reapers had left. The men who were reaping always left a little for the poor people, because the Lord had commanded the reapers not to take all away, but to leave a little for the poor. And Ruth and Naomi were poor. Therefore, Ruth asked her mother-in-law to let her glean in some field where the man would give her permission to do it.

Naomi said to her, "Go, my daughter."

Now, Naomi had a kinsman at Bethlehem who was named Boaz. He was a rich and great man. Ruth happened to come into the field that belonged to Boaz. There she gleaned after the reapers.

Boaz came out to the field and spoke to his reapers. "The Lord be with you," he said to them.

They answered him, "The Lord bless you."

Then he asked his chief servant, "Whose young woman is this?"

The servant answered, "It is the young woman that came with Naomi out of the land of Moab. She said to us, 'I pray you let me glean after the reapers,' and we allowed her to do it. So she came into the field and hath kept on gleaning from the morning until now."

Then Boaz spoke kindly to Ruth. He told her not to go into any other man's field, but to glean in his, for he had commanded his young men to do her no harm. When she was thirsty, he said, she should go to the pitchers which the young men had filled and drink what she wanted. Ruth bowed down to the ground before Boaz and asked why he was so kind as to take notice of a stranger. Boaz answered that he had been told of all her kindness to her mother-in-law—how she had left her father and her mother and the land where she was born, and had come to live among the children of Israel.

He asked that God might reward her, because she had done these things.

Boaz told her to come at mealtime and eat and drink with the reapers, and she did as he said and sat beside them. Boaz handed her parched corn, and she ate and had enough. Afterward she went out in the field again. Boaz commanded his young men to let her glean, even among the sheaves that they had bound up for him. He said, "Let fall some handfuls on purpose for her, that she may take them, and do not find fault with her."

So she gleaned in the field until evening. Then she beat out the grains of barley that she had gathered and took them and went into Bethlehem. When her mother-in-law saw how much Ruth brought, she was glad. She asked the Lord to bless the man who had been so kind to her. And Naomi asked her who the man was.

Ruth said, "The man's name is Boaz." Then Naomi told her that he was a near kinsman to them. Ruth said he had asked her to come again into his field and glean after the reapers, and to do so until they had ended all of his harvest. Naomi told her to do as Boaz said.

So she went out into his field every sunny day and gleaned there until the end of the barley harvest and of the wheat harvest.

Naomi said to Ruth, "Boaz winnows barley tonight in the threshing floor." Barley is a grain something like wheat. To thresh it was to separate it from the long straw on which it grew. To winnow it was to separate it again from the small, broken pieces of straw which were left mixed with it after the threshing. These pieces could not be picked out with the hands, as there were too many of them. Instead, the reapers would throw the grain and the small pieces of straw together, up in the air, while the wind was blowing. The wind would blow away the straw, because it was so light, but the grains of barley, being heavier, would fall down by themselves in a heap on the ground. The threshing floor was the smooth, level piece of ground where these things were done.

Naomi had heard that Boaz was to winnow his barley that night. She asked Ruth to wash and dress herself, then go to the threshing floor. There she was to speak to Boaz the words which she told her.

Ruth did as her mother-in-law said. She washed and dressed herself and went to the threshing floor. Boaz winnowed his barley, and then he had a feast. After he had eaten and drunk and had enough, she came near to him and spoke to him, saying, "You are our near kinsman." She asked him to be kind to her.

He answered, "May the Lord bless you, my daughter." Then he told her not to fear. He would do for her all that she needed, he said, because all the people of Bethlehem knew that she was a virtuous and good woman. He said to her, "Bring your veil here and hold it out."

And when she brought it, he poured into it six measures of barley.

Ruth carried it to Naomi and told her all that Boaz had done, saying, "These six measures of barley he gave me, for he said, 'Go not away without taking something with you for your mother-in-law.' " Naomi told Ruth to wait and be patient until she should see what else Boaz would do.

We have read that the cities of Canaan had walls around them with gates. It was at the gate that the people used to meet together. Whoever came into the city or went out of it passed through one of them. That was the place where the rulers came to hold their court and try those who disobeyed the laws and say what their punishment must be. Persons also bought and sold things at the gate, making a kind of market there. When any man wanted all the people to know of something he was going to do, he would go and speak about it at the gate, for there he found more of them gathered together than anywhere else.

The day after Boaz had winnowed his barley, he went to the gate of Bethlehem and sat down in a seat there. He called to him ten of the elders, or principal men, of the city and said to them, "Sit down here."

They sat down.

Then Boaz spoke to them, and to all the people, and told them that he was going to take Ruth, the daughter-in-law of Naomi, to be his wife. He said to the elders and to all the people, "You are the witnesses. That is, you are the persons to whom I tell it, that you may know it yourselves and tell others, also."

All the people and the elders answered, "We are the witnesses." And they prayed that the Lord would bless Ruth and make Boaz still richer and greater than he was then.

So Boaz took Ruth, and she was his wife. Naomi was glad for her daughter-in-law who had loved her and had come with her out of the land of Moab into Canaan to live with the children of Israel and serve the Lord.

Jonah

NINEVEH WAS ONE of the mightiest cities of the old
times. In it were temples, palaces, and houses for
a great multitude of people. There were also beautiful
gardens and green fields where cattle were fed. Around
the city were walls a hundred feet high. These walls were
so thick that on their top three chariots drawn by horses
might be driven side by side. Towers were built above
the walls, all around the city. There were fifteen hundred
towers, each one being two hundred feet high. On the top of
the walls, and in the towers, the Assyrian soldiers stood.
They shot arrows and darts at their enemies. But Nineveh
was a very wicked city.

God spoke to the prophet Jonah, saying, "Arise and go
to Nineveh, that great city, and tell the people of the
punishment that is coming upon them for their sins."

Jonah did not want to go, so he fled to Joppa, a city by the sea. There he found a ship that was going to a far country. Jonah paid his fare and went into it so that he might flee to someplace where he would not hear the Lord speaking to him.

When he had sailed out on the sea, the Lord sent a strong wind and a great storm, and the ship was in danger of being broken to pieces. The sailors were afraid. They prayed, each one to his idol, for help, and they threw out some of the loading of the ship to lighten it and keep it from sinking. But Jonah did not know of the danger they were in, for he had gone down to the lower part of the ship and lay there fast asleep through the storm.

The captain came to him and awakened him, saying, "What are you doing, O sleeper? Rise up and pray to your God. Perhaps He may pity us and save us from perishing."

The men said to one another, "Because someone in the ship has done wickedly, this storm is sent. Come, let us cast lots that we may find out for whose sake it is brought upon us."

So they cast lots, and the lot fell on Jonah. They said to him, "Tell us, what wicked thing have you done? Where is your own country? And to what people do you belong?"

Jonah answered, "I am a Hebrew and am fleeing from the Lord who made the sea and the dry land so that I may not hear His voice speaking to me."

The men were greatly afraid. "Why have you done this thing?" they asked Jonah. "What shall we do to you so that the sea may be still for us?"

Jonah answered them, "Take me up and cast me into the sea. Then shall the sea be still for you, because I know that it is for my sake this danger has come upon you."

But the men did not want to throw him into the sea.

They rowed hard to bring the ship to land, but could not. Then they prayed to the Lord, whom Jonah had told them of. They cried out to Him, saying, "O Lord, we beseech Thee, punish us not for casting this man into the sea, as if we were putting to death one who had done us no harm, for Thou, O Lord, has sent the storm on his account."

They took up Jonah and cast him into the sea, and the sea grew still and calm. The men wondered, and they offered a sacrifice to the Lord. Then they promised, after that, to serve Him.

Now, the Lord had sent a great fish to the side of the ship to swallow up Jonah as soon as he should be cast into the sea. The fish swallowed Jonah, and he was in the fish three days and three nights. While he was in the fish, he prayed to the Lord. He cried to God in his trouble, confessing his sin. God heard him and forgave him at last. He commanded the fish to cast him out on dry land.

Then the Lord spoke to him a second time, saying, "Rise up and go to Nineveh, that great city, and preach to the people the words that I shall tell thee."

So Jonah arose and went. He came into the middle of the city, which was as far as he could walk in one day. There he cried out with a loud voice, "After forty days Nineveh shall be destroyed for the sins of the people."

When the people and the king of Nineveh heard this, they believed that God had sent Jonah, and that the words he spoke would come true. The king rose up from his throne. He took off his royal robes and put on sackcloth. Then he and his princes sent word through the city that all the people should fast. "Let not man nor beast," they said, "eat any food or drink any water, but let them be covered with sackcloth. Let everyone pray with all his heart and cease doing wickedly, for who can tell but the Lord may forgive us and take His great anger from us so that we perish not."

When God saw how they prayed to Him and ceased doing evil, He took away His anger from them and did not destroy the city.

Samuel

THERE WAS A MAN of the children of Israel named Elkanah. He went every year from the city of Ramah,
where he lived, to offer up a sacrifice at the tabernacle in
Shiloh. His wife, whose name was Hannah, went with
him. Elkanah loved his wife and gave her a present whenever he went to offer up his sacrifice. Yet she was unhappy,
for the Lord had given her no child.

She came to the tabernacle and prayed and made a vow
to the Lord that if He would give her a son she would
give that son back to Him; he would be a Nazarite and
would be set apart to serve the Lord all the days of his
life. While she prayed she wept. Eli was the high priest
at that time. Eli saw her lips moving, but he could not
tell what she said, for she spoke softly so that her voice
was not heard.

"Go in peace, and may God give you what you ask him for," Eli said to her kindly.

Hannah was glad at the high priest's words. She went away and looked sad no more. She and her husband left Shiloh and went back again to their home in the city of Ramah.

The Lord remembered Hannah's prayer and sent her a son. She called his name Samuel, which means "Asked of God," because she had asked God for him, and God had given him to her.

When Samuel grew old enough, she took him up to the tabernacle and she brought him before Eli. Then she and her husband offered a bullock as a sacrifice. Hannah spoke to Eli, saying, "O my Lord! I am the woman that stood by you here, praying unto the Lord. For this child I prayed, and the Lord has given me what I asked Him for. Therefore, I have given the child back to the Lord. As long as he lives, he shall be given to the Lord." And she left Samuel to stay with Eli at the tabernacle.

Eli had two sons. Their names were Hophni and Phinehas, and they were priests at the tabernacle. The Lord had said that the priests should be holy because they were His ministers who offered up sacrifices to Him. But Hophni and Phinehas were not holy. They were wicked men.

When any man offered up a peace offering, only a part of it was burned on the altar. The rest was given away —some of it to the priest, for him to eat, and some of it to the man who brought the offering, for him to eat. But Hophni and Phinehas took more than their share of the peace offerings. If any man was unwilling for them to have so much, they would take it from him by force. Therefore, the people did not care to come anymore to the tabernacle with their offerings.

Samuel, who was only a child, did what was right. He pleased the Lord. His mother made him a little coat and brought it up to him each year when she came up with her husband to offer sacrifice. Eli spoke kindly to them. He asked the Lord to bless them because they had given Samuel to the Lord. His parents came every year to Shiloh and worshipped, and afterward they went away again to their own home. But Samuel stayed with Eli at the tabernacle.

Now, Eli was very old. When he heard of the evil things which his sons did, he said to them, "Why do you such things?" He was grieved at their wickedness, yet he did not punish them nor put them away from being priests, as he ought to have done, but allowed them to go on in their sin.

There came a prophet to him with a message from the Lord. The Lord asked why he allowed his sons to take the best part of all the offerings the people brought. Eli cared more to please his sons, the Lord said, than he did to please Him. Therefore, the Lord declared, He would not have Eli for His high priest, but would choose another man who should do His will. Both of Eli's sons, the Lord said, should die in one day.

Samuel stayed at the tabernacle, doing as he was bidden by the high priest. One night he lay down to sleep, and Eli lay down, also. Soon Samuel heard a voice calling to him. "Here am I," he answered. He rose up and ran to Eli and said that he had come because Eli called him. But Eli said, "I called not; lie down again." So Samuel went and lay down once more.

When he heard the voice again, he arose and went to Eli and said, "Here I am, for you called me."

Eli answered, "I called you not, my son; lie down again."

When Samuel heard the voice a third time, he went to Eli and said, "Here I am, for you did call me."

Eli knew then that it was the Lord who had called the child. Therefore, he said to him, "Go, lie down. If He calls you, say 'Speak, Lord, for Thy servant heareth.'"

So Samuel went and lay down. And the Lord came and called as before, "Samuel, Samuel."

Samuel answered, "Speak, Lord, for Thy servant heareth."

Then the Lord told him that He was going to do a thing which would make everyone who should hear of it afraid. He would punish Eli and his sons as He had said, because his sons had made themselves wicked, and Eli had not kept them from doing so. Even though they would offer up sacrifices and burnt offerings for their sins, He would not hear them nor forgive them.

When the Lord was done speaking, Samuel lay still until the morning. Then he rose up and opened the doors of the tabernacle. He was afraid to tell Eli of what the Lord had said. But Eli called him and asked him, "What is the thing that the Lord has said unto you? Hide it not from me. God do so to you if you hide anything from me of all that the Lord has spoken."

Then Samuel told him every word. He hid nothing from him. When Eli heard it, he said, "It is the Lord. Let Him do what He must."

And Samuel grew, and the Lord blessed him, and all the people knew that he was chosen to be a prophet.

Samuel Anoints David

WHEN SAMUEL GREW up, he was a priest in the temple for many years. Always he did as God commanded him.

One day God told Samuel that he should go to the city of Bethlehem, to a man named Jesse, and anoint one of Jesse's sons to be king.

Samuel answered, "How can I go? If King Saul hears of it, he will kill me."

The Lord told Samuel to take a heifer to offer up as a sacrifice, and to ask Jesse to come to the sacrifice. Afterward, the Lord told him, He would show him what he should do.

Samuel did as he was commanded. He came to Bethlehem and made ready his sacrifice, and he invited Jesse and his sons to come to it. When they came, Samuel thought that Jesse's oldest son was the one whom the Lord had chosen for king. But the Lord told him he was not the one. Then Jesse called another, but the Lord did not choose him, either. Jesse called seven of his sons to pass before Samuel, but Samuel said, "The Lord has chosen none of these."

Then Samuel asked, "Are these all your children?"

Jesse had one other son, whose name was David. He answered, "There is yet one left, the youngest, but he is keeping the sheep."

Samuel said, "Send and bring him."

They sent and brought him. He had been out in the field, and when he came in and stood before them his cheeks were red and his face was beautiful to look at.

The Lord said to Samuel, "Arise, anoint him, for this is he."

Samuel took oil and poured it on his head, anointing him before all his brothers. Thus the Lord chose David to be king over Israel. But he was not to be king at once, or for a long while afterward.

Now, an evil spirit went into Saul and troubled him. Saul's servants told him that he should look for a man who could play well on the harp. When the evil spirit troubled him, they said, that man should come and play before him. Then the evil spirit would go away.

Saul said to his servants, "Get for me now a man that can play well."

One of them answered that he had seen such a man. He was the son of Jesse, the Bethlehemite. It was David of whom he spoke, for David knew well how to play on the harp.

Therefore, Saul sent messengers to Jesse and told him to send David, his son, who kept the sheep. Jesse took an ass and loaded it with bread, a bottle of wine and a kid and sent them by David as a present to Saul, but he did not let Saul know how Samuel had anointed David to be king. So David came to Saul and stayed with him and waited on him, for he pleased him well. When the evil spirit troubled Saul, David took a harp and played with his hand and made sweet music that comforted him. Then the evil spirit went from Saul. But after a while, David left Saul's house and returned to his own home. Saul had many other servants, and he forgot David.

David and Goliath

O NE TIME THE Philistines gathered together their armies
to fight against Israel. Saul and the men of Israel
made ready for the battle. The camp of the Philistines
was on a mountain on one side. The camp of Israel was on
a mountain on the other side. There was a valley between
them.

There came out of the camp of the Philistines a giant.
He was named Goliath of Gath. On his head was a helmet
made of brass, and he wore a coat of armor. Pieces of
brass covered his legs so that no sword or spear might
wound him. He came into the valley between the two
armies, where the men of Israel could see him, and cried
to them, "Choose you a man out of your army, and let
him come down to me. If he be able to fight with me and
to kill me, then we will be your servants. But if I kill

115

him, then shall you be our servants. I defy the armies of Israel this day. Give me a man, that we may fight together."

When Saul and the men of Israel heard these words, they were greatly afraid. No man in Saul's army was willing to go out and fight with the giant.

Every morning and evening for forty days he came out and defied all the men of Israel. But still no man of Israel dared to fight this man.

Now, David was feeding his father's sheep at Bethlehem, but his three elder brothers had gone out with Saul to fight against the Philistines.

One day Jesse said to David, his son, "Take now this parched corn and these ten loaves of bread, and run to the camp, to your brothers. Carry these ten cheeses as a present to their captain, and see how they do."

David rose up early in the morning, left the sheep with a servant, and went toward the army camp to find his brothers as his father commanded.

He came to the camp just as the host was going out to fight. The Philistines and the children of Israel had made ready, and now they stood, one army before the other. All the men shouted for the battle.

David left the things he had brought with a man, and he ran into the army to speak with his brothers.

While he talked with them, Goliath came out between the two armies and spoke the same words that he had spoken before. This time David heard him. The men of Israel fled from him in fear. David heard them say that if any man would kill the Philistine, the king would give him great riches and also the king's daughter to be his wife. David then asked them to tell him again what would be done for the man who would kill the giant of the Philistines.

Eliab, David's eldest brother, heard him asking. He was angry with him and said, "Why did you come down here? Who have you left at home to take care of the sheep? I know the naughtiness of your heart, for you have come down to see the battle."

But David answered his brother, saying, "What wrong have I done? Who is this Philistine, that he should defy the armies of the living God?" David called the armies of Israel the armies of God, because the children of Israel were God's chosen people. He called God the living God, because all other gods were only dead idols.

When the men who were near him heard the words that David spoke, they told them to Saul, and Saul sent for him.

David told Saul that he would go out against the Philistine. David said, "Let no man's heart be afraid because of him. I will go and fight with this Philistine."

Saul said to him, "You are not able to go out against him, for you are but a youth, and he has been a man of war from his youth."

David answered, "While I was keeping my father's sheep, there came a lion, and a bear, and took a lamb out of the flock. I went after the lion and struck him and set the lamb free from his mouth. When he rose against me, I caught him by the beard and slew him. I slew both the lion and the bear. This wicked Philistine shall be like one of them, seeing he has defied the armies of the living God. The Lord who saved me from the paw of the lion and the paw of the bear will save me from the hand of this Philistine."

And Saul said to David, "Go, and the Lord be with you."

Then Saul gave David his own armor, his helmet of brass, his coat of mail, and his sword.

But David said, "I cannot go with these."

So he put them aside and took his staff, such as shepherds carried. He chose five smooth stones out of the brook and put them in his shepherd's bag. With his sling in

117

his hand, he came near to the Philistine.

When the Philistine saw David, he thought him not worth fighting, for David seemed not like a soldier, strong and brave, such as Goliath expected would come out against him, but like a shepherd boy, gentle, and with a beautiful face, who had never before seen a battle.

The Philistine said, "Am I a dog, that you come to me with a staff?" He called on the idols that he worshipped to curse David, and he told him to come near that he might kill him.

David answered, "You come to me trusting in your sword, your shield, and your spear. I come to you trusting in the God of Israel."

When the Philistine came near, David made haste and ran toward him. He put his hand in his shepherd's bag and took out a stone. He slung it and struck the Philistine in his forehead, so that the stone sunk into it. The Philistine fell down upon his face to the earth.

So David overcame the Philistine with a sling and a stone, for there was no sword in his hand. He ran and stood upon the Philistine and took his sword from him and killed him.

When all the Philistines saw that the man in whom they trusted was slain, they fled.

David was proclaimed a great hero, and Saul took him to live at the palace.

Solomon's Wisdom

FOR MANY YEARS David ruled the people of Israel wisely and well. When he died, his son, Solomon, was made king.

Solomon loved God and was careful to do no evil. God spoke to him in a dream one night and offered him anything that he desired to have. God said to him, "Ask what I shall give thee."

Solomon answered, "Give Thy servant an understanding heart to judge Thy people, that I may know what is good and what is bad. For who is able to judge this Thy so great a people?"

God was pleased with the answer that Solomon made. He told him that because he had not asked for riches or a long life or victory over his enemies, He would give him the wisdom he asked for, and besides this, riches and honor, more than any of the kings who had been before him or who would be after him.

God also promised that if he would obey His commandments He would give him a long life, also.

Here is one example of Solomon's wisdom:

Two women who lived together in one house came to King Solomon and stood before him. One of them spoke to the king, saying, "O my lord, this woman and I live in one house, and each of us had a little son. This woman's child died in the night, and she rose up at midnight, while I slept, and took my son from me and laid it in her bed, then laid her dead child in my bed. When I woke in the morning to feed my child, it was dead, but when I looked upon it, I saw it was not my child."

After this woman was done speaking, the other contradicted her, saying, "No, the living child is my son, and the dead is yours."

The king called out to his servants, "Bring here a sword!" And they brought it.

Then the king said, "Cut the living child in two, and give half to one and half to the other."

Then the true mother of the child, because she loved it and would not have it killed, said, "O my lord, give her the living child and on no account slay it."

But the other, who pretended to be its mother, said, "Yes, cut it in two."

Then the king commanded that the child should be given to the woman who had pity on it, because he knew that it must be hers. It was to find out which woman was the true mother that he called for the sword, not because he intended to slay the child.

All the people heard of what the king had done, and they served him, because they saw that God had given him wisdom to judge fairly.

Elijah

MANY KINGS RULED over Israel. Some were good and some were cruel. When Ahab was made king, he set up an image of a heathen god, Baal. He built temples to the god and commanded the people to worship Baal.

The Lord was displeased with Ahab. He sent the prophet Elijah to tell him that there would not be any more rain in the land of Israel for many years. No rain would come there, the Lord said, until Elijah asked for it. As this would make Ahab very angry at Elijah, the Lord told the prophet to flee where Ahab could not find him.

"Go," the Lord said, "and hide by a brook that is in the wilderness. Thou shalt drink of the water of the brook. I have commanded the ravens to bring food to thee there."

So Elijah went and hid by the brook. He drank of the water, and the ravens brought him bread and meat in the morning and bread and meat in the evening. But after a while, because there had been no rain, the brook dried up. A great famine came to the land.

Then the Lord said to him, "Arise and go to the city of Zarephath, for I have commanded a widow woman there to feed thee."

Elijah arose and went. When he came to the gate of the city, the widow woman was there gathering sticks. He called to her, "Bring me, I pray you, a piece of bread."

She answered, "As surely as the Lord God lives, I have no bread, but only a handful of meal in a barrel and a little oil in a cruse. Now I am gathering a few sticks that I may go in and bake it, for me and my son to eat."

Elijah said to her, "Fear not. Go and bake it, as you have said, but make a little cake for me first and bring it. After that make more for you and your son. The Lord says that although there is but little of the meal and of oil, yet they shall last until He sends rain upon the earth."

The woman did as Elijah commanded. Afterward she and her son ate for a whole year, and the Lord made the meal and the oil last all that time.

After this the son of the woman grew sick. His sickness was so great that he died. When she told Elijah of it, he said, "Give me your son."

Elijah took him out of her arms, carried him into his own chamber, and laid him on his bed. Then he cried out to the Lord, "O Lord, hast Thou brought evil upon the woman in whose house I stay, by slaying her son? I beseech Thee, let the child's soul come into him again."

The Lord heard Elijah's prayer. He sent the soul of the child into him again, and he lived. Elijah took him and brought him down out of his chamber and gave him to his mother.

After the famine had lasted for more than three years the Lord spoke to Elijah, "Go, show thyself to King Ahab, and I will send rain on the land."

Elijah started to go. But Ahab did not know that Elijah was coming or that the Lord was going to send rain. He called Obadiah, his chief servant, and said to him, "Go and look wherever there are any brooks or springs of water. Perhaps we may find grass enough there to save the horses and mules." Ahab and Obadiah went out to search for food and water all through the land.

Ahab went one way by himself, and Obadiah went another way by himself.

As Obadiah went on his way, he met Elijah. Obadiah knew him and fell on his face. "Are you my lord Elijah?" he asked.

Elijah answered him, "I am. Go tell King Ahab that Elijah is here."

Obadiah answered, "There is no nation or kingdom where Ahab has not sent to seek for you. As soon as I have gone to tell him that you are here, the Lord will carry you away, I know not where, and hide you. When Ahab shall come and cannot find you, he will kill me."

But Elijah answered, "As surely as the Lord lives, I will show myself to Ahab this day."

So Obadiah went and told Ahab, and Ahab came to meet Elijah. When he saw him, he said, "Are you the man who troubles the people of Israel?"

But Elijah answered, "I am not the one who troubles Israel. It is you and your family, because you have forsaken the Lord and served Baal."

Elijah told Ahab to gather all the people at Mount Carmel, including all the priests, or prophets, of Baal—four hundred and fifty men.

Ahab sent word to all the people, and gathered them and Baal's prophets together at Mount Carmel. Elijah came there and spoke to the people, "How long will you be in deciding whom you will serve? If the Lord be God, obey Him; but if Baal be God, then obey him."

The people heard what Elijah said, but they remained

silent and answered him not a word.

Elijah said, "Bring two bullocks. Let Baal's prophets choose one of them and kill it and lay it on Baal's altar, but not put any fire under it. I will take the other bullock and kill it and lay it on the Lord's altar, and not put fire under it. They shall pray to Baal to send down fire from heaven, and I will pray to the Lord. The one that sends down fire to burn up his offering, he shall be God." And all the people answered that it should be as Elijah said.

Baal's prophets chose their bullock and killed it and laid it on the wood on the altar, but put no fire under it. Then they cried out to their idol from morning till noon, saying, "O Baal, hear us!" And they leaped up and down at their altar and lifted their arms to it.

But no voice answered them. Neither did any fire come down and burn up their offering.

About noon Elijah mocked them and said, "Call louder upon your god, for perhaps he is talking to someone and cannot hear, or has gone away from his home on a journey, or is asleep and must be awaked."

They cried to Baal until the evening. They cut themselves with knives till the blood gushed out, hoping it would make their idol answer them. But no answer came.

Then Elijah called all the people to come near him, and they came near. He took twelve stones and built up the altar of the Lord which had been broken down, and he made a trench around it. He put the wood on the altar, then cut the bullock in pieces and laid it on the wood. "Fill four barrels with water and pour it on the burnt sacrifice and on the wood," he said to the people.

When they had done it, he said, "Do it a second time." And they did it a second time. Then he said, "Do it a third time." And they did it the third time. The water ran down over the sacrifice and over the wood. It filled the trench around the altar.

In the evening, at the time when the priests at the

temple offered up a lamb for a burnt offering, Elijah came near to the altar and prayed to the Lord, saying, "Hear me, O Lord, hear me, so that this people may know Thou art the true God, and that Thou dost call them from serving idols to serve Thee again."

The fire of the Lord fell from heaven upon the altar and burnt up the bullock and the wood and the stones of which the altar was made. It licked up the water that was in the trench.

When all the people saw it, they fell on their faces and said, "The Lord, He is God! The Lord, He is God!"

Elijah said to them, "Take the prophets of Baal. Let not one of them escape."

Elijah spoke to King Ahab and told him that now he might go and eat and drink, for the rain was coming and the famine would soon be ended. So Ahab went to eat and drink at a place a little way off on the mountain.

Elijah went up to the top of Mount Carmel. He kneeled down with his face to the ground and prayed that God would send rain. After he had prayed, he said to his servant, "Go up now and look toward the sea."

The servant went up to a place still higher on the mount and looked. He came back and said, "I see nothing."

Elijah said, "Go again seven times."

After the seventh time he came, saying, "There rises up out of the sea a little cloud as large as a man's hand."

Elijah then knew that the Lord was sending the rain. So he said to his servant, "Go, say unto Ahab, 'Make ready your chariot and get down from the mountain, lest the rain stop you.'"

While Elijah's servant was going, the little cloud rose up from the sea. It grew larger, until all the sky was black with clouds and wind, and there was a very great rain. Ahab rode in his chariot and went to the city of Jezreel. The Lord gave Elijah strength to run before the chariot till he came to the gate of the city.

Elisha Cures Naaman

THE ISRAELITES WERE once at war with the Syrians. At that time many women and children were taken to Syria to serve the people there. A little girl was brought to the house of Naaman, the captain of the army of the Syrians, to wait upon the mistress of the house.

Naaman was a great man with his master, Benhadad, king of Syria, because he had gone out to war against the king's enemies and had gained the victory over them. Naaman was also a mighty and brave soldier, but he was a leper, which means he suffered from a terrible disease called leprosy.

One day the little maid said to her mistress, "I wish that my master could see the prophet that is in Samaria, for he would cure him of his leprosy."

When Benhadad heard this, he said to Naaman,

"You shall go to Samaria, and I will give you a letter to the king of Israel who lives there."

Naaman went, taking with him ten talents of silver, six thousand pieces of gold, and ten changes of raiment, so that he might have a present for the man who should make him well. When he came to the city of Samaria, he took the letter to Jehoram, king of Israel.

Benhadad's letter said, "I have sent Naaman, my servant, to you, that you may cure him of his leprosy."

When the king of Israel had read the letter, he was troubled. He rent his clothes and said to his servants, "Have I the power of God, that I can cure this man of leprosy? See, how Benhadad is seeking for an excuse to make a quarrel against me."

When the prophet, who was Elisha, heard that the king was troubled, he sent word to him, saying, "Why have you rent your clothes? Let the man come now to me, and he shall know that there is indeed a prophet in Israel."

Naaman came with his horses and his chariot and stood at the door of the house of Elisha. Elisha sent out a messenger to him, who said, "Go, wash seven times in the River Jordan, and you shall be clean." He meant that Naaman would be well.

But when the messenger came to Naaman and told him these words, he was angry. "I thought the prophet would surely come out to me himself and pray to the Lord his God and put his hand upon me and make me well," he said. "Are not the rivers in my own country better than all the rivers in the land of Israel?" He turned and went away in a rage.

His servants came near to him and said, "My father, if the prophet had bid you do some hard thing that you might be made well, would you not have done it? How much better, then, it would be to obey him when he tells you only to wash and be clean."

Naaman went down and dipped himself seven times in

the river Jordan. His flesh grew pure and clean as the flesh of a little child, and he was made well of his leprosy.

He and all the men who were with him went back to the house of Elisha. There Naaman said, "Now I know there is no other God in all the earth but the God of Israel."

Then he said to Elisha, "I pray you take a present from your servant."

But Elisha answered, "As surely as the Lord lives, I will take no present from you."

Naaman begged him, but he would not.

Daniel, Shadrach, Meshach, and Abednego

AT ONE TIME Nebuchadnezzar came up from Babylon in Chaldea and besieged Jerusalem and conquered Israel.

He commanded the chief of his officers to choose some of the princes of the children of Israel to be servants in his palace at Babylon. None should be chosen, the king said, who had any fault in them, but only such as were young and handsome and quick to learn, for he wanted them to learn all the wisdom of the Chaldeans and also the language that the Chaldeans spoke. After they had been instructed in these things for three years, they were to live at the palace and wait on the king.

Among those that were chosen by the chief officer were four young men. Their names were Daniel, Shadrach, Meshach, and Abednego. They were brought to Babylon, and teachers were set over them so that they might be taught as King Nebuchadnezzar commanded. Each day the king sent them meat and wine from his own table, intending so to feed them until they should come to live at the palace and wait upon him.

The Chaldeans worshipped idols and offered up sacrifices of animals and gifts of wine to them. They ate of the sacrifices and drank of the wine that had been offered to their idols. But Daniel did not wish to eat what had been offered to idols, lest he might offend the Lord. Besides, some of the animals that the Chaldeans ate, the Lord had commanded the children of Israel not to eat. The animals were called unclean. Therefore, Daniel said to himself, he would not eat of the meat nor drink of the wine that the king sent him. The three young men who were with him said they would not, either.

Daniel spoke to the chief officer, who had the care of him, about this thing and asked his permission not to eat the food which the king sent. The Lord had made the chief officer love Daniel, yet he dared not do as Daniel asked him.

He answered, saying, "I am afraid it will displease the king, who sends you your meat and your drink, for if, after a while, he should see that your faces look paler and thinner than the faces of the other young men who eat food from the king's table, he may be angry with me and put me to death."

The chief officer gave Daniel and his friends to the care of the steward. Daniel asked the steward for permission not to eat the food. He said, "Try us, I beseech you, for ten days. Give us for that time only vegetables to eat and water to drink. Afterward, look at our faces and at the faces of the other young men. If we do not look as well as they do, then give us whatever you think best to eat."

The steward gave them vegetables for ten days. At

the end of that time their faces were fatter and fairer than the faces of all the other men who ate food from the king's table. Then the steward took away the meat and the wine that were sent to them and gave them only vegetables to eat. God helped these four young men to acquire knowledge and wisdom, and He made Daniel understand visions and dreams.

After they had been taught for three years, the chief officer brought them into the palace of the king. King Nebuchadnezzar talked with them and found that among all those who had been chosen for his servants, none were like Daniel, Shadrach, Meshach, and Abednego. Therefore, they stayed at the palace and waited on the king. In all the questions which the king asked them concerning the things they had learned, he found them ten times better than all the wise men in his kingdom.

The king made Daniel a great man and gave him many great gifts. He made him ruler over the whole province of Babylon and also chief of the governors over all the wise men of Babylon. The king set Shadrach, Meshach, and Abednego to watch over the affairs of the province of Babylon.

But Daniel sat in the gate of the king.

One time Nebuchadnezzar made an image of gold and set it up on a plain in the province of Babylon. Then he called the princes, the governors, the captains, the judges, and all the rulers of his kingdom. When these great men gathered together before the image that Nebuchadnezzar had set up, one of the king's servants called out in a loud voice to them, "It is commanded that as soon as you hear the sound of the harp, the flute, the trumpet, and all kinds of music, you shall fall down and worship the golden image that Nebuchadnezzar, the king, has set up. Whosoever does not fall down and worship shall that same hour be cast into the midst of a burning, fiery furnace."

The king then commanded the musicians to play. As

soon as the people heard the sound of music, they all fell down and worshipped the golden image.

Some of the Chaldeans came to the king and spoke against the Jews, saying, "O King, live forever! You have made a law that every man who shall hear the sound of the flute, the harp, the trumpet, and all kinds of music shall fall down and worship the golden image and that whosoever does not fall down and worship shall be cast into the burning, fiery furnace. There are some Jews whom you have set over the province of Babylon, named Shadrach, Meshach, and Abednego. These men, O King, have not obeyed you. They serve not your gods nor worship the golden image which you have set up."

Because these men had not obeyed him, Nebuchadnezzar commanded that Shadrach, Meshach, and Abednego be brought to him.

When they were brought before the king, he said, "Is it true, O Shadrach, Meshach, and Abednego, that you do not serve my gods nor worship the golden image that I have set up? If you are ready when you hear the sound of the harp, the flute, the trumpet, and all kinds of music, and fall down and worship the image I have made, no harm shall be done to you. But if you worship not, you shall be cast, the same hour, into the midst of a burning, fiery furnace. Who is the God that is able to save you out of my hands?"

Then Shadrach, Meshach, and Abednego answered. They said to the king, "We are not afraid to tell you what we will do in this matter. If you cast us into the burning, fiery furnace, our God, whom we serve, is able to save us from death. He will save us out of thy hand, O King. Yet even if He let us burn, we tell you, O King, that we will not serve your gods nor worship the golden image that you have set up."

Nebuchadnezzar was full of fury. He looked in fierce anger on Shadrach, Meshach, and Abednego. He said to his servants that they should heat the furnace seven times hotter than it was heated before. He commanded the most mighty soldiers in his army to bind Shadrach, Meshach, and Abednego, and cast them into it. The men were bound, in their coats, their hats, and their other garments, and thrown into the burning, fiery furnace. Because the furnace was exceedingly hot, and the king made them go near it, the flames killed the men who cast Shadrach, Meshach, and Abednego in. As for Shadrach, Meshach, and Abednego, they fell down, bound, into the midst of the fire. But soon they rose up and walked in the fire, for God would not let it burn them.

Nebuchadnezzar, the king, was astonished. In haste he said to the rulers and great men who were with him, "Did we not cast three men bound into the midst of the fire?"

They answered, "We did, O King."

Then he said, "Lo, I see four men loose and walking in the midst of the fire. They are not hurt. The form of the fourth is like the Son of God."

Nebuchadnezzar came near the mouth of the burning, fiery furnace. He cried out, "Shadrach, Meshach, and Abednego, you servants of the Most High God, come here."

Shadrach, Meshach, and Abednego came out of the midst of the fire. The princes, governors, and captains who were gathered together saw these men whom the fire had not hurt. Not a hair of their heads was burned. Neither were their coats changed. There was not even the smell of the fire upon them.

Nebuchadnezzar said, "Blessed be the God of Shadrach, Meshach, and Abednego, who has sent His angel and saved His servants that trusted in Him. Therefore, I make a decree and a law: Every nation and people which shall speak evil of the God of Shadrach, Meshach, and Abednego shall be destroyed, and their houses shall be torn down and made into heaps, for there is no other God that can perform such works."

The king made Shadrach, Meshach, and Abednego greater than they had been before in the province of Babylon.

Daniel Explains a Dream

W HEN BELSHAZZAR REIGNED over the kingdom of Baby-lon, he gave a feast in his palace for a thousand of his lords.

While they were feasting and making merry, there came a man's hand which wrote words upon the wall in the room where the king and his lords held their feast. The writing was in a language they could not understand. When the king saw the hand that wrote, his face was changed and his knees trembled and smote one against another. His thoughts troubled him and he was filled with fear. He cried out aloud for his servants to bring in the wise men before him.

When the wise men came, he said to them, "Whoso-ever shall read this writing and tell the interpretation of it shall be clothed with scarlet and have a chain of gold about his neck and shall be the third ruler in the kingdom."

But none of the wise men could read the writing or tell the interpretation. The king was troubled even more.

When the queen heard what the king had said, she came in before him and spoke to him, saying, "O King, live forever. Let not your thoughts trouble you, nor let your face be sad. There is a man in your kingdom in whom is the spirit of the holy gods. In the days when your father, Nebuchadnezzar, lived, great wisdom was found in him. Your father made him master over all the wise men of Babylon, because he had knowledge and understanding for interpreting dreams and telling of secret things. Let Daniel be called, and he will tell the interpretation."

Then was Daniel brought before the king. The king spoke to him, "Are you that Daniel who was brought captive with the children of Israel, out of Judah? I have heard of you that the spirit of the gods is in you, and that you have understanding and excellent wisdom. The wise men have been brought in before me to read this writing and make known to me the interpretation, but they cannot. I have heard of you that you can interpret and tell secret things. Now, if you can read the writing and make known the interpretation of it, you shall be clothed with scarlet and have a chain of gold about your neck and shall be the third ruler in the kingdom."

Daniel answered the king, "Keep your gifts for yourself and give your rewards to another. Yet will I read the writing to the king and make known to him the interpretation. O King, the most high God gave Nebuchadnezzar, your father, a kingdom and glory and honor. And because God made him so great, all nations trembled and feared before him. Whom he would he slew, and whom he would he put down.

"When his heart was full of pride so that he forgot God, he was made to come down from his throne. His greatness was taken from him. He was driven out from his palace and from living among men. He was made like the beasts and lived with the wild asses. They fed him grass like oxen. His body was wet with the dew till he learned that God rules over the nations of the earth and makes whomsoever He will to be king.

"And you, his son, have not humbled your heart, though you knew all this, but have been proud and sinned against God. They have brought the vessels of his temple before you, and you and your lords and your wives have drunk wine in them. You have praised the idols of silver and gold, of brass, iron, wood, and stone, which cannot see, nor hear, nor know anything. The true God who lets you live and gives you all things, you have not praised. Therefore has He sent this hand, and this writing was written. These are the words of it: MENE, MENE, TEKEL, UPHARSIN. This is the interpretation: Your kingdom is ended. God has taken it from you. He tried you as king, but you have not obeyed Him. He has given your kingdom to the Medes and the Persians."

When Daniel had interpreted the writing, Belshazzar commanded his servants to clothe him with scarlet and put a chain of gold about his neck. The king then made a decree that he should be the third ruler in the kingdom. That same night came Cyrus with the army of the Medes and Persians into Babylon, and Belshazzar, the king of the Chaldeans, was slain, and Darius, the Mede, took the kingdom.

Daniel and the Lions

WHEN DARIUS, THE MEDE, was made king, it pleased him to set over the people one hundred and twenty princes. Over these princes he set three presidents. Daniel was the first of them. He was the chief of all the presidents and princes because of the wise and good spirit that was in him.

The presidents and the princes hated Daniel because he was greater than they, and they tried to find out some evil concerning him so that they might speak against him to the king. They could find none, however, for he was faithful and no fault or error was to be found in him.

Therefore, these men said, "We shall not be able to complain of Daniel to the king, unless it be something he does in serving his God."

They gathered together and came to the king. "King

Darius, live forever," they said. "All the presidents of your kingdom, the governors, the princes, and the captains, want a law and a decree to be made that for thirty days whosoever shall ask help of any god or man, except of you, O King, shall be cast into the den of lions. Now, O King, make this law and decree and sign the writing so that it cannot be changed, for the law of the Medes and Persians changes not." King Darius signed the writing and the decree.

When Daniel knew that the writing was signed, he went into his house. The windows of his chamber being opened toward Jerusalem, he fell upon his knees three times a day and prayed and gave thanks to his God, as he had always done.

The presidents and the princes gathered together and found Daniel praying and asking help of God. They went to the king and said, "Have you not signed a decree that whosoever shall ask help of any god, or man, for thirty days, except of you, O King, shall be cast into the den of the lions?"

The king answered, "The decree is signed and is made a law of the Medes and Persians, which changes not."

They answered, "Daniel, who is one of the captives of Judah, obeys you not, O King, or the decree that you have made. He prays and asks help of his God three times a day."

When the king heard these words, he was displeased with himself for having made the decree, because he did not want to punish Daniel. He set his heart on having him excused. He tried until evening to save him from punishment. But the presidents and the princes gathered together and said to the king, "You know, O King, that the law of the Medes and Persians is that no decree or law which the king has made can be changed."

At last King Darius commanded his servants to cast Daniel into the den of lions. The king said to Daniel, "Your

God whom you serve continually will deliver you."

The king went home to his palace and would eat no food. The instruments of music were not played before him as at other times. He could not sleep. He arose very early in the morning and went in haste to the den of lions and cried with a mournful voice unto Daniel, "O Daniel, servant of the living God, is your God, whom you serve continually, able to deliver you from the lions?"

Daniel answered the king, "O King, live forever. My God has sent His angel and shut the lions' mouths that they have not hurt me, because I have not sinned against Him. Also, unto you, O King, I have done no wrong."

The king was exceedingly glad for him, and he commanded that they should take Daniel up out of the den. When Daniel was taken up, no hurt was found upon him, because he trusted in his God.

King Darius then wrote to all people and nations of the earth, saying, "I make a decree that in every part of my kingdom men tremble and fear before the God of Daniel, for He is the living God. His kingdom is the one that shall not be destroyed, and His power shall never end. He is the God who can save from danger, who has saved Daniel from the mouths of the lions."

Daniel prospered in the reign of Darius, and in the reign of Cyrus, who was made king after Darius was dead.

Esther

Many, many years ago King Ahasuerus ruled over the land of Persia. At one time he sent messengers throughout the kingdom telling the officers to gather all the beautiful young women at his palace at Shushan so that he might choose the one he liked best as his queen.

There was among the servants at the palace a Jew named Mordecai. He had a cousin named Esther who was a Jewess. Her father and mother were dead. When they died Mordecai took Esther to his house, and he had brought her up as his own daughter. The maid was fair and beautiful.

When the king's commandment was made known through the land, many young maidens were gathered together at the palace at Shushan. Esther was brought there among them and given to the care of the king's officer who had charge of the women. The officer was pleased with Esther. He gave her a present and also seven young maidens to wait on her, and he put her and her maidens into the best part of the house of the women. Esther did not let it be known that she was a Jewess, for Mordecai had advised her not to tell it.

When King Ahasuerus saw Esther, he loved her more than all the other maidens who were brought before him. He set the royal crown upon her head and made her queen. He made a great feast that was called Esther's feast, and he gave gifts to his servants for her sake. Esther was still careful to do all that Mordecai told her. Although she was made queen, she obeyed Mordecai as willingly as when she lived in his house as his daughter.

In those days, two of the king's officers, because they were angry with the king, wanted to lay hands on him and kill him. Mordecai, who was a watchman at the king's gate, heard what they said. He told Esther, and Esther told the king. When the officers were examined, their guilt was found out, and they were both hanged on a gallows. What Mordecai had done to save the king's life was written down in a book where an account was kept of all the principal things that happened in the kingdom.

Now, there was at the palace a servant named Haman. King Ahasuerus made Haman a great man; he set him above all the princes at the palace. All the king's servants who watched by the king's gate bowed down and did reverence before Haman, for so the king commanded them to do.

But Mordecai would not bow down before him. The king's servants said to Mordecai, "Why do you not obey the king's commandment?" After they had spoken to him several times, and he still would not listen to them, they told Haman of it.

When Haman saw that Mordecai neither bowed nor did him reverence, he was very angry. He determined to punish Mordecai. But he was not satisfied to punish Mordecai alone; he wanted to punish and destroy all the Jews who were in Persia, for the king's servants had told him that Mordecai was a Jew. Haman spoke to King Ahasuerus against the Jews.

He said, "There are some of them living in all the provinces of your kingdom. They have laws of their own which are different from the laws of your people. Neither do they obey the king's law. Therefore, it is not well for the king to let them live. If the king will make a decree that they will be destroyed, I will pay ten thousand talents of silver into the king's treasury."

King Ahasuerus listened to what Haman said. Then he took a ring from his finger and gave it to Haman. The ring was what the king used when he made a law or a decree; he sealed the writing with his ring instead of signing it with his name, as we do now. That was what made it one of the laws of the Medes and Persians which could not be changed. When he gave Haman his ring, he meant that Haman should make such a decree as he chose against the Jews and seal it with his ring. It would be the same as if the king himself had made it. The king also told Haman that he need not pay the ten thousand talents of silver into his treasury.

Haman called the king's scribes, or writers, together. They wrote for him a decree that, on the thirteenth day of the twelfth month, the people of Persia should kill and destroy all the Jews in the kingdom, both young and old, little children and women. Whoever should kill them had permission to take their houses, their lands, and their money, and to keep these things for his own. Haman sealed the decree with the king's ring, and copies of it were sent by messengers to the governors and rulers of all the provinces so that it might be made known to all the people of Persia. The messengers went out in haste, according to the king's commandment.

When Mordecai heard of the decree that Haman had made, he was filled with sorrow. He rent his clothes and put on sackcloth. He went out into the streets of the city and cried with a loud and bitter cry. He came even before the king's gate, although he might not pass through there, because it was forbidden that anyone should pass through the king's gate who was clothed in sackcloth.

In every province where the messengers brought the decree, there was great mourning among the Jews. Many lay down in sackcloth and ashes, because of their grief.

Queen Esther had not yet heard of the decree. When her maids came and told her that Mordecai was clothed in sackcloth, and that he cried in the streets of the city. Esther was very sorry. She sent new garments to him, that he might take off the sackcloth and put the new garments on. But he would not. Therefore, Esther sent one of the king's officers to Mordecai to ask why he was troubled. The officer went to the street before the king's gate, where Mordecai was, and asked him. Mordecai told the officer of all that had happened and of the money that Haman had promised to pay into the king's treasury if he might be allowed to destroy the Jews. Mordecai also gave the officer a copy of Haman's decree to show Esther, and he asked the officer to tell the queen that she should go to the king and beseech him to save the Jews.

When the officer told Esther what Mordecai said, she sent word to Mordecai, saying, "All the king's servants and all the people of Persia know that whosoever shall go in before the king without being called, whether it be man or woman, must be put to death unless the king shall hold out the golden scepter. But I have not been called to come unto the king these thirty days. How, then, can I go and speak with him?"

The officer told Mordecai. But Mordecai sent again to Esther and said to her, "Do not think because you are queen that our enemies will spare you when they kill all the Jews. If you will not try to save your people at this time, someone else shall save them. But you and your relatives shall be destroyed. Who can tell whether you have not been made queen on purpose for this time, so that you might save them?"

Then Esther sent word to Mordecai, saying, "Go and gather together all the Jews that are in the city. Let them fast for me, neither eating or drinking for three days, night or day. I and my maidens will fast, also. Then I will go in and speak with the king, although he has not called for me. If I be put to death, I am willing to die."

Mordecai called all the Jews together, and they did as Esther commanded.

On the third day Esther dressed herself in her royal robes and went into the inner part of the king's palace and stood where the king, as he sat on his throne, could see her. When he saw her, God made him feel kindly toward her, and he held out his golden scepter to her. She came near to him and touched the top of the scepter.

Then the king said to her, "What is your desire, Queen Esther, and what is your request? It shall be given to you, even to the half of my kingdom."

Esther answered, "If the king be willing, I want the king and Haman to come today to a banquet that I made ready for him."

The king said to his servants, "Tell Haman to make haste, that he may do as Esther has said." The king and Haman came to the banquet that Esther made ready.

The king knew that Esther had invited him because she wanted to ask some favor of him. As they sat at the banquet, he said to her again, "What is your desire? It shall be given to you, even to the half of my kingdom."

Esther answered, "My desire is that the king and Haman come to another banquet which I shall make ready for them tomorrow, if the king be willing. Then I will tell the king what it is I would ask of him."

So the king and Haman went to the queen's house that day. Haman's heart was filled with pride because he had been to the queen's banquet and was invited to her house again on the morrow. But as he went out and passed Mordecai at the king's gate and saw that he did not bow to him nor do him reverence, he was filled with anger. But he said nothing.

When he came to his home, he called for his friends and for his wife. Haman boasted to them of his riches and greatness. He told them how the king had set him above all the princes and the king's other servants.

He said also, "And Esther the queen allowed no man to come in with the king to the banquet excepting myself. Tomorrow I am invited to come again with the king to her house. Yet all these things cannot make me happy while I see Mordecai, the Jew, sitting in the king's gate."

Then his wife and all his friends said to him, "Let a gallows be made, fifty cubits high. Tomorrow ask the king that Mordecai be hanged on it. After that, go merrily to the queen's banquet."

Haman was pleased with what they said to him. He went out and commanded the gallows to be made.

That night the king could not sleep. He told his servants to bring him the book in which was written down an account of the principal things that had happened in his kingdom. When the book was brought before him, it was found written that Mordecai had, a long while before, saved the king's life by telling of two of the king's officers who had intended to kill him.

Then King Ahasuerus said to his servants, "What reward has been given Mordecai, or what honor has been done to him, because he did this?"

They answered, "There has been nothing done for him."

While the king was speaking to his servants, someone came into the court of the palace. "Who is it in the court?" the king asked.

It was Haman who had come there that he might ask the king's permission to have Mordecai hanged on the gallows which was made ready for him. The king's servants answered, "It is Haman who stands in the court."

The king said, "Let him come in."

When Haman came in, the king said to him, "What shall be done for the man whom the king wants greatly to honor?"

Then Haman said to himself, "The king means me. I am the one whom he wants greatly to honor." Therefore, he answered the king, "Let the royal robes that the king wears, the horse that he rides, and the crown that is set on his head be brought to the man whom the king wants greatly to honor. Let him wear the king's robes and his crown, and let him ride upon the king's horse. Let one of the king's most noble princes lead the horse through the streets of the city and cry out to all the people, 'Thus shall it be done to the man whom the king delights to honor!'"

Then the king said, "Make haste and take the robes and the horse and the crown and do to Mordecai, the Jew, as you have said. Leave nothing that you have spoken undone."

Because he dared not disobey the king, Haman took the king's robes and his horse and his crown and brought them to Mordecai. Then he led Mordecai on horseback through the streets of the city, crying out before him to all the people, "Thus shall it be done to the man whom the king delights to honor!"

After all this, Mordecai came and humbly sat down in his place at the king's gate. But Haman made haste to his home, full of shame and with his face covered, so that no one might know him. He told his wife and all his friends what had happened to him. While he was talking with them, the king's messenger came to bring him to the banquet that Esther had made ready.

At the banquet the king said again to Esther, "What is your petition, Queen Esther? What is your request? It shall be given to you, even to the half of my kingdom."

Esther answered, "If the king be pleased with me, this is my request: that the king will save my life and the lives of all the Jews. Evil things which are not true have been spoken against us, and I and my people have been sold to be destroyed, to be slain, and to perish."

"Who is the man that has dared to do these things?" King Ahasuerus asked.

Queen Esther answered, "Our enemy is the wicked Haman."

Haman was suddenly afraid before the king and queen. The king arose from the banquet in great anger and went out into the palace garden. When he came again into the banquet room, Haman had fallen down before the queen to beg for his life.

One of the king's officers said to the king, "Behold, the gallows, fifty cubits high, which Haman made ready for Mordecai, who saved the king's life, is standing by the house of Haman."

The king said, "Hang him upon it."

They hanged Haman on the gallows that he had made ready for Mordecai. The king's anger went from him.

On the same day King Ahasuerus gave to Esther the house in which Haman had lived. Mordecai was called in before the king, for Esther told him that Mordecai was her relative, and how kind he had been to her. The king took off his ring, which he had before given to Haman, and gave it to Mordecai. And Esther made Mordecai ruler over the house that had belonged to Haman.

Esther was still troubled, however, because the decree which Haman had written and sealed with the king's ring had been sent out to all the provinces telling the governors, the rulers, and the people of Persia that on the thirteenth day of the twelfth month they should kill and destroy the Jews in every city and take away whatever belonged to them. Therefore, Esther came again to the king, though he had not called for her. She fell down at his feet and wept there. Then the king held out the golden scepter toward her. She arose and stood before him and begged that the decree of Haman might be changed, for, she said, "How can I bear to see my people perish?"

Now, the king himself could not change the decree which he had allowed Haman to make, because, as we have read, no decree of the Medes and Persians might ever be changed. But King Ahasuerus told Esther and Mordecai that they might make another decree concerning the Jews and seal it with the king's ring.

Mordecai called the king's scribes together and commanded them to write another decree. This decree said that the Jews had permission, on the thirteenth day of the twelfth month, to gather themselves together in every city and to slay and destroy all who should try to harm them.

Mordecai sent copies of this decree to the different provinces of the kingdom. The messengers went out in haste, according to the king's commandment.

After he had finished talking with the king, Mordecai came out from the palace clothed in royal garments of blue and white, such as the king himself wore, and with a crown of gold upon his head. All the people of Shushan were glad. Everywhere the Jews were filled with joy, and they feasted and were happy.

On the thirteenth day of the twelfth month the Jews took their swords and gathered themselves together in every city to fight for their lives. They gained the victory over all who came out against them. On the fourteenth and fifteenth days they rested from fighting against their enemies.

God saved Esther and her people from those who had hoped to destroy them. Esther and Mordecai sent letters to all the Jews telling them to keep the fourteenth and fifteenth days of the twelfth month, every year, as a time of feasting and gladness. At that time they should rejoice together and give presents to one another and gifts to the poor, because they had once been saved from their enemies, and their sorrow and mourning had been turned into joy.

Between
the Old and the New
Testaments

BETWEEN THE STORIES in the Old and New Testaments, a period of about four hundred years passed. The Bible tells us nothing of the life of the Jews during this time. From other books we learn that they continued to be servants to the kings of Persia for a long time. Then Alexander, a great general who was at war with Persia, brought an army and took Jerusalem. The Jews served him for nine years.

Later they lived under the rule of Egypt and Syria. Some of the rulers were kind. Others treated the Jews cruelly, killing some, taking many captives, and ransacking the temple and carrying away the treasures that were kept there.

At last the Romans came with an army. They took Jerusalem and broke down its walls. The Jews were made servants to the Romans.

The Romans sent a general named Herod to be their king. He was not one of the children of Israel, yet he pretended to believe in their religion and to worship God as they did. He was, in truth, a fierce and cruel man who cared only to keep all the power to himself.

After he had been king eighteen years, finding that the Jews despised him for his wickedness, he determined to build up the temple of the Jews anew. By doing this he hoped to please the Jews and make them more willing to have him rule over them. The temple which then stood on Mount Moriah was nearly five hundred years old. It was much broken and decayed. Herod took it down, a part at a time, and built it up again with great stones of white marble. These stones he covered, in some places, with plates of silver and gold. The building was very splendid. It shone brightly under the morning sun.

The inside of the temple was divided into two rooms, as it had been before, by the curtain called the veil. One of the rooms was the holy place, where the golden altar, the golden table, and the golden candlestick stood; the other was the most holy place, where the ark used to stand. But the ark had been lost long before (we suppose) when the Jews were carried captive to Babylon because of their sins. Now they had no ark to bring into the most holy place; it was empty except for a stone which lay where the ark should have been.

Outside of the temple was a court called the court of the priests. There stood the altar of burnt offering and the laver. Outside of this court was another court. It was called the court of Israel, where the men of Israel might come. Beyond this was a third court called the court of women, because the women of Israel might go there. Outside of this, and around all the others, was a very large court called the court of the Gentiles, because the Gentiles—that is, the people of other nations besides the

Jews—were allowed to go into it.

Nine large and splendid gates opened into these courts. One, more splendid than the rest, was called the Beautiful Gate. It was seventy-five feet high and covered with Corinthian brass, which at the time was more costly than silver or gold. Around the different courts, walls were built; the wall around the court of the Gentiles was twenty-five feet high. On the inside of this wall were wide porches with flat roofs; they rested on marble pillars so large that three men with their arms stretched out could hardly reach around one of them. The floor of the porches was paved with different colored marble. One of the porches was called Solomon's, because it stood over a very high wall which Solomon had built up from the valley below. These porches made a beautiful covered walk for the people in hot or stormy weather; in pleasant weather they walked upon their flat roofs, from which they had a view of the temple, the city, and the mountains that were around Jerusalem.

The Jews did not go into the temple itself to worship. Only the priests were allowed to go there. The people worshipped in the courts of the temple; when they said they were going up to the temple, they meant they were going up to its courts. The way up to these, on the top of Mount Moriah, was by high flights of steps.

Herod had eighteen thousand men at work on the temple and its courts. It took him over nine years to build them.

John the Baptist

WHILE HEROD WAS king in Judea there lived a priest named Zacharias. His wife was named Elizabeth. The Bible tells us that they were righteous and careful to obey all God's commandments. They were both very old, but God had never given them a child.

Every day, before the priests began their work, lots were cast for them to see what part of the work, or service, each one was to do.

One day Zacharias was to burn incense at the hour of prayer.

While he was in the temple he saw an angel standing beside the golden altar. When he saw the angel he was afraid.

The angel said, "Fear not, Zacharias, for God will give you and your wife, Elizabeth, a son. You shall call him

John. He shall not drink wine or any strong drink and shall be filled with God's Holy Spirit from the time he is born. He shall tell the children of Israel of the Savior who is coming. He shall teach many of them to repent of their sins and obey him."

Zacharias was filled with wonder and said to the angel, "But how shall I know that these things will be?"

The angel answered, "I am Gabriel, who stands in the presence of God. I am sent to speak unto thee and to tell thee these glad tidings.

"And, behold, thou shalt be dumb and not able to speak until the day that these things shall be performed, because thou believeth not my words, which shall be fulfilled in their season."

The people who were waiting in the courts of the temple for Zacharias to come out of the holy place wondered what kept him so long. When he came, they saw that he could not speak. But he made them understand, by signs, that he had seen a vision.

God gave to Zacharias and Elizabeth the son He had promised them. When the child was eight days old, their neighbors and relatives came together to dedicate him to the Lord, and also to decide what his name should be. And they called him Zacharias, after the name of his father. But his mother said, "No. He shall be called John."

They said to her, "None of your relatives are called by this name."

They asked Zacharias what he would have the baby called. Zacharias asked for a writing table, because he could not speak, and wrote, "His name is John."

They were all astonished, for Zacharias had not yet told them that the angel had given him this name in the temple.

As soon as Zacharias had written these words, God gave him power to speak again. He spoke and praised God. When the people in that part of the land heard of what had been done, they said to each other, "What sort of child shall this be?"

The boy grew, and the Lord blessed him. He lived in the lonely wilderness, away from the rest of the people, until he was a man. Then the time came for him to preach to the Jews and tell them about the Savior. For this little child, whom God had given to Zacharias and Elizabeth, was John the Baptist.

The Birth of Jesus

THE ANGEL GABRIEL came one day and spoke to a young maiden named Mary.

He said, "God has greatly blessed thee. Thou shalt have a Son and shalt call His name Jesus. He shall be great and shall be the Son of God. And of His kingdom there shall be no end."

So Mary waited for this blessed event to take place. She went to her home in Nazareth where she lived with Joseph, her husband.

Meanwhile, the emperor of Rome made a decree that all the world should be taxed. He commanded everyone to go to be taxed in the city where his fathers had lived. Therefore, everyone went to his own city.

Mary, with Joseph, her husband, went out of Nazareth, where their home was then, to Bethlehem, where David used to live, because they were descended from King David.

When they came to Bethlehem, there was no room at the inn, so they went into the stable to sleep. While they were there, God gave to Mary the son which the angel had promised her. It was in the stable in Bethlehem that the infant Jesus was born. And Mary His mother wrapped Him in swaddling clothes and laid Him in a manger.

In the country there were shepherds who stayed out all night in the field watching over their flocks. That night the angel of the Lord came down to them, and a bright light shone around them. The shepherds were afraid when they saw him.

But the angel said, "Fear not, for, behold, I bring you good tidings of great joy, which shall be to all people. For unto you is born this day, in the city of David, a Savior, who is Christ the Lord. And this is the way you shall know Him: You shall find the Babe wrapped in swaddling clothes and lying in a manger."

When the angel had said this, suddenly there was a multitude of angels with him. They praised God, saying, "Glory to God in the highest and on earth, goodwill toward men."

After the angels had gone from them up into heaven, the shepherds said to one another, "Let us go now to Bethlehem and see these things of which the angel has told us."

They came with haste, and found Mary and Joseph and the Babe lying in a manger. Afterward they went out and told others what the angel had said to them about the Child. All whom they told wondered at what they said. Then the shepherds returned to their flocks again, praising God for what they had seen and heard.

When the Babe was eight days old, His parents called His name Jesus, as the angel had commanded, and they dedicated Him to the Lord.

After this Joseph and Mary brought Him to Jerusalem. They took Him to the temple and offered up a sacrifice, as it was written in the law of the Lord.

There was a man in Jerusalem named Simeon. He was a good man who loved God. He expected Jesus to come into the world as the prophets had promised, for the Lord had promised Simeon that he should not die until he had seen Jesus. On the day that Joseph and Mary brought Jesus to the temple, the Lord told Simeon to go into the temple. When Joseph and Mary brought in the Child, Simeon took Him up in his arms and said, "Now, Lord, Thy promise has come true. I can die in peace, because I have seen the Savior."

There was a woman named Anna, a prophetess. She was a widow of great age. She lived near the temple so that she might worship there day and night. While Simeon was speaking, Anna came into the temple where Jesus was. She thanked God because He had let her see Him. Then she went out and spoke of Him to others who were looking for the coming of the Savior.

When Jesus was born in Bethlehem, there came to Jerusalem wise men from a far-off eastern country. They asked the people, "Where is He that is born to be King of the Jews? We have seen His star in the sky and are come to worship Him."

The people answered, "In the city of Bethlehem, for so the prophet has said."

As the wise men hurried toward Bethlehem the star which they had seen in their own land appeared to them again. When they saw the star, they were filled with joy, for it moved on before them until it came and stood over the house where the young Child was. When they went into the house and saw the Child with Mary, His mother, they bowed down and worshipped Him.

In those days, persons who came to visit kings brought presents with them. The wise men brought presents for

161

Jesus. They brought such things as were precious in the country where they lived. When they had opened these things, they gave to Him gifts of gold, frankincense, and myrrh.

The Boy Jesus

JOSEPH AND MARY went every year to Jerusalem to keep the feast of the Passover. When Jesus was twelve years old, He went with them.

After the feast was ended, they started on their journey back to Nazareth. Now, people who went to the Passover traveled in companies; friends and neighbors would go to Jerusalem together. Some of them rode on mules and horses, but many of them walked all the way. It was with such a company that Joseph and Mary started to return to Nazareth. They thought that Jesus was among those who journeyed with them, so they went on till evening. When they looked for Him, they could not find Him.

They left the company they journeyed with and went back to Jerusalem at once. They had been one day in coming to the place where they missed Him; it took them one day more to go back to Jerusalem. On the third day they found Him at the temple, talking with the wise men—hearing what they said and asking them questions.

All who heard Jesus were astonished at the things that He spoke, for He was only a child and those whom He talked with were men of great learning.

His mother said to Him, "Son, why hast Thou treated us so? Thy father and I have been looking for Thee, anxious and sorrowful."

He answered, "Why have you looked for Me? Did you not know that I must be about My Father's business?"

He meant that He must be doing what His Father in heaven had sent Him on earth to do. God had sent Him to teach men and explain the Scriptures to them. But Joseph and Mary did not understand what He meant by the words that He spoke to them.

Jesus returned with His parents to their home in the city of Nazareth, and He lived with them and obeyed them. And as He grew, God blessed Him, and those who were with Him loved Him.

The Baptism of Jesus

THE BIBLE TELLS us nothing more about Jesus, or about John the Baptist, for many years. During those years Jesus lived with His parents in the city of Nazareth, and He grew to be a man. The people did not know that He was the Son of God, and John the Baptist had not yet preached to them about Him.

John was still living in the wilderness. His clothes were made of the coarse hair that grows on the back of the camel. They were fastened around his waist by a girdle or belt of leather. For his food he had locusts, which he found in the wilderness, and the honey which the wild bees left among the rocks and in the hollow trees.

The time had now come for John to preach to the people. God commanded him to go and tell the people to make ready for the Savior by repenting of their sins.

165

John went into the lonely country near the River Jordan, and a great multitude came there to hear him. He preached to them and told them that the Savior, who had been promised, was soon coming among them, and that He would save the righteous but destroy the wicked. The Jews must not think, John said, that their sins would be forgiven because they were descended from a good man like Abraham. They must obey God themselves. Many who heard John preach repented. They were baptized by him in the River Jordan.

John said to the people who came out to hear him, "I indeed baptize you with water, but the Savior who is coming after me is greater than I. He will baptize you with the Holy Ghost."

John meant to tell the people that although he baptized them with water, he could not wash away their sins; but that Jesus, because He had power to send the Holy Spirit into their hearts, could really wash away their sins for them.

Jesus came out from His home in Nazareth for John to baptize Him. When John saw Him he did not wish to baptize Him. John said, "I have need to be baptized by Thee. Dost Thou come to be baptized by me?"

John felt that he had need to have his own sins washed away. But Jesus had no sins to be washed away. Why, John wondered, should He be baptized? It was because Jesus had come on earth to obey all of God's commandments.

When John refused to baptize Jesus, Jesus told him that although he could not understand it now, it was right that he should baptize Him. John consented and went down with Him into the River Jordan. He baptized Jesus there.

While Jesus was coming up out of the water, praying to God, the sky above Him opened, and there came down from heaven what seemed to be a dove. It lighted on

Him. It was the Holy Spirit that came down in the form of a dove.

At the same time God's voice spoke out of heaven. God said, "This is My beloved Son, in whom I am well pleased."

Jesus Goes to a Wedding

ONCE JESUS WENT into the city of Cana, which was in a part of the land called Galilee. There was a marriage in the city of Cana, and both Jesus and His disciples were invited to the marriage. The mother of Jesus was there, too. A feast was made ready for all the guests. Food was prepared for them to eat, and wine for them to drink. Before the end of the feast, however, the wine was all gone.

When the guests wanted more, the mother of Jesus said to Him, "They have no wine."

Then she said to the servants, "Whatever He tells you to do, do it."

Now, there were in the house six waterpots made of stone, which the Jews kept to hold water. Jesus said to the servants, "Fill the waterpots with water." The servants

168

filled the containers up to the brim.

Then He said, "Take some out now and carry it to the man who is in charge of the feast." When they did so, the water was changed into wine.

But the governor, the man in charge of the feast, did not know that Jesus had changed it into wine. Therefore, when he tasted of the water that had been made wine he called the bridegroom to him and said, "When other people give a feast, they set the good wine on the table first. After men have had enough, they bring out that which is worse. But you have kept the good wine until now."

This was the first miracle that Jesus did to show His power to the people. When His disciples saw it, they believed that He was the Son of God.

Jesus Begins His Ministry

Jesus and his disciples went into a part of the land called Galilee. On the way they came to a city named Sychar. Just outside of the city was a well, called Jacob's well, where the people came to get water. It was in the hot part of the day, and Jesus, wearied from His journey, sat down by the well. His disciples had gone into the city to buy food and had left Him alone.

A woman came out of the city carrying her pitcher to draw water. Now, this woman was a sinner. She did not love God in her heart and had done many things to displease Him. Jesus knew this, for He sees all our hearts and knows of everything that we have done. He talked with the woman and told her of some of the things she had done, long ago, to displease God.

She was surprised, and she said, "Sir, I see Thou art a

prophet." She meant that He was a person whom God told of things which other people did not know. She said to Jesus, "I know that the Savior is coming into the world. When He comes He will tell us all things."

Jesus said to her, "I who speak to thee am He."

The woman left her pitcher and made haste back to the city. She said to the people, "Come and see a man who told me all things that I ever did. Is not this the Savior?"

The people went out and saw Jesus. They begged Him to come into their city. He came and stayed with them three days. They listened to the things that He taught them. Then they said to the woman, "Now we believe in Him, not because you told us about Him, but because we have heard Him ourselves and know that He is the Savior who has come down from heaven."

From that time Jesus began to teach all the people in the land of Israel, telling them that the day of judgment was coming and that they should repent of their sins and believe in Him.

After this Jesus went again to the city of Cana, where He had changed the water into wine. A nobleman who lived in another city came to Him and begged Him to heal his son, who was very sick.

The nobleman said, "Sir, come quickly, before my child dies."

Jesus said to him, "Go to thy home. Thy son is made well."

The man believed what Jesus said. He left at once to go to his home, as he was told. Before he reached there, however, his servants met him and said to him, "Your son is well."

He asked at what time he began to get better. They answered, "Yesterday at the seventh hour the fever left him." The man knew that it was at the same hour when Jesus said to him, "Thy son is made well." The nobleman and all his family believed that Jesus was the Son of God.

171

Some Miracles

WHEN JESUS WENT down to Capernaum, which was a city by the Sea of Galilee, great numbers of people came there to hear Him. As He stood by the sea, they crowded upon Him. He saw two boats on the shore, but the fishermen had gone out of them and were mending their nets. Jesus went into one of the boats, which was Peter's, and asked him to push it out a little way from the land. He sat down and taught the people from the boat.

When He had finished teaching them, He said to Peter and to Andrew, his brother, "Sail out now on the sea, and let down your nets into the water to catch fish."

Peter answered, "Master, we have been laboring all night and have caught nothing. Yet, at Thy command, I will let down the net."

When they had done this, they caught a great multitude of fishes—so many that the net broke. They beckoned to their partners, who were in the other boat by the shore, that they should come and help them. They came and filled both boats with the fish until the boats began to sink.

When Peter saw the miracle which Jesus had done, he was astonished, and so were his partners, James and John. Peter kneeled down and worshipped Jesus, saying, "I am a sinful man, O Lord."

Jesus did this miracle so that these men might see it and believe in Him and know that He was the Son of God. He had chosen the fishermen to be His disciples and to go with Him wherever He should go. He said to them, "Come with Me." They left their boats and their nets and all that they had, and they followed Him.

In the morning, rising up even before it was light, Jesus went out to a lonely place in the wilderness. There He prayed to God.

After He had gone, the people came to Peter's house seeking Him. Peter and the other disciples looked for Jesus, and when they found Him, they said, "All the people are seeking Thee."

Jesus answered, "I must go and preach the gospel in other cities, also." He went through all Galilee, teaching in the synagogues and preaching the gospel to the people.

There came to Him a man with leprosy. The man kneeled down before Him and said, "Lord, if Thou wilt Thou canst make me clean."

Jesus pitied him and put out His hand and touched him. "I will. Be thou clean," He said.

Immediately the leprosy went from him, and he was made clean. Jesus sent him away, commanding him to tell no man who had healed him, but to go to the priest at the temple and offer up a sacrifice, as Moses had commanded those persons who were cured of leprosy. But the man told all the people what Jesus had done for him.

When Jesus went again into the city of Capernaum, the people gathered together at the house where He was, and He preached to them.

The houses of the Jews were usually square, and one story in height. The roofs were flat, with railings around them, so that persons might safely walk there. In the center of the house was a large square room called the court. Over this the roof was left open, but in time of rain or heat, an awning was stretched across the opening.

It was in such a house as this that Jesus had now come. Some men brought to the house a man who was sick and unable to walk. They wanted Jesus to heal him. When they could not come in at the door because of the crowd, the men went up on the roof. Taking off the covering, they let the man down on his bed into the room below, where Jesus was.

When Jesus saw how much faith the men had, He said to the sick man, "Thy sins are forgiven. Stand up on thy feet and take up thy bed and go to thy house."

Immediately the man rose. He stood on his feet and took up his bed and went out before them all.

The people who saw it were astonished.

We have read that the Jews had to pay tribute money, or taxes, to the Romans. There were men in each city who took these taxes from the people. They were called publicans. The Jews hated them, not only because they collected money for the Romans, but also because most of them were unjust and cruel men, taking more than was right. Not all the publicans did this, however.

As Jesus passed by, He saw one of them, named Matthew, sitting at the place where the people came to pay the tribute money. Jesus said to him, "Follow Me." Rising up, Matthew left all and followed Jesus. From that time he was one of His disciples.

Soon afterward there was a feast of the Jews, and Jesus went up to Jerusalem. There was at Jerusalem by the sheep gate a pool of water called the Pool of Bethesda. Around it were built five porches. In the porches lay a great number of persons who were sick, blind, or lame. They waited there, because at certain times the water moved, as if someone had stirred it. They thought that whoever went into it first, after it was troubled, was made well of whatever disease he had.

A man was there who had been sick for thirty-eight years. Jesus saw him and, knowing how long he had been sick, pitied him. He said to him, "Wilt thou be made well?"

The man answered, "When the water is troubled, I have no one to help me into the pool. While I am trying to get down to it, another one always steps in before me. I am always too late."

Jesus said to him, "Rise, take up thy bed and walk." Immediately the man was made well. He took up his bed and walked.

Now it was the Sabbath day. The Jews, wishing to find fault, said to the man, "It is wicked for you to carry your bed on the Sabbath."

The man answered, "He that cured me told me to take up my bed and walk."

They asked him, "Who is it told you?"

The man said it was Jesus. Then the Jews began to persecute Jesus, saying He had broken the Sabbath day.

Jesus told the Jews that the miracles which He performed showed that God had sent Him into the world.

On another Sabbath day when Jesus went into the synagogue, a man was there whose hand was withered so that he could not open it or stretch it out. The Pharisees watched Jesus to see whether He would heal the man on the Sabbath. They were anxious to accuse Him of doing wrong. Jesus knew their thoughts, and He said to them, "If one of you have a sheep which should fall into a pit on the Sabbath, would you not lay hold of it and lift it out? And if it be right to do good to a sheep, how much more is it to do good to a man! Therefore, I tell you, it is right to do good on the Sabbath day."

Then He turned to the man and said, "Stretch out thy hand." The man stretched it out, and it was made well like the other.

The Pharisees were filled with madness against Him. They left the synagogue and talked with one another about some way of putting Him to death. When He knew of it He left that place, with His disciples, and came to the Sea of Galilee. When they heard of the wonderful works that He did, many persons from Jerusalem and Judea and from far-off countries came to Him. Those who were sick crowded around Him so that they might touch Him and be made well. He healed them all.

Jesus Chooses Twelve Disciples

ONCE JESUS WENT out to a desert place alone and stayed there all night praying to God. When it was morning He called His disciples to Him. He chose twelve of them that they might be with Him and that He might send them out to preach and give them power also to do miracles—to heal those that were sick and to cast out devils. These twelve He called apostles, which means messengers. They were Peter and his brother Andrew, James and his brother John, Philip and Bartholomew, Thomas and Matthew the publican, James and Thaddeus, Simon and Judas Iscariot.

Seeing the multitudes that followed Him, Jesus went up onto a mountain. When He sat down, His disciples came to Him, and He taught them there. He told them what persons were truly happy; He said:

"Blessed are the poor in spirit, for theirs is the kingdom of heaven.

"Blessed are those who mourn, for they shall be comforted.

"Blessed are the meek, for they shall inherit the earth.

"Blessed are those who hunger and thirst after righteousness, for they shall be filled.

"Blessed are the merciful, for they shall obtain mercy.

"Blessed are the pure in heart, for they shall see God.

"Blessed are the peacemakers, for they shall be called the children of God."

Jesus told his disciples that when they were treated cruelly and persecuted for His sake, they should not be sorry, but glad, for great would be their reward in heaven. They were not the only ones, He said, who had been treated so. Even the prophets, the holy men whom God had sent long ago, were treated in the same way.

He said to His disciples that they must let their lights shine; He meant they must not be afraid to let others know that they loved and obeyed God. Instead of hiding this, they must let others see it. By their example others might be led to love and obey God, also. Jesus said that if we do the things which God commands and teach others to do them, we shall be called great in the kingdom of heaven. But if, like the scribes and Pharisees, we teach those things without doing them, we cannot enter into the kingdom of heaven.

He said to the people, "Your teachers have told you that if you kill another person, you are in danger of being punished. I tell you that if you are even angry with another who has done you no harm, you are in danger of punishment."

Jesus told His disciples that when they were going to the temple to worship God, they must try to remember whether they had done wrong to any other person—

whether they had taken anything that belonged to him, or had said what was not true about him, or in any other way had done him harm. If they had, they must go and do what was right to that person. God would not accept their worship while there was some sin in their hearts of which they had not repented.

We must be pure and good, Jesus said, in all we do and say. We must not even think an impure or bad thought.

When others are unkind to us and do us harm, we must not do harm to them in return. Instead, we must do good to them and pray for them and love them. Then, Jesus says, we will be children of our Father in heaven. He is even kind to those who do not obey Him or love Him. We must try to be like Him—perfect in all things.

Jesus commanded His disciples to be careful, lest they should do what is right only because they wanted others to see them and praise them. This was not the reason that they should do right. They should do it because they wanted to please God. When they gave anything to the poor, they should not go about telling of it. When they prayed to God, they should not choose a place where others could see them; they should go into their chamber and shut the door, so that no one but God could see them. Then God would answer their prayers.

When they fasted, they should not look sad, as the hypocrites did, to let others know they were fasting; they should look as cheerful then as at other times, so that no one but their heavenly Father would know they were fasting. Then their heavenly Father would reward them.

Jesus said that we must not want to be rich and to lay up a great deal of money in this world. We must lay up riches in heaven. He did not mean that we could lay up money in heaven; we shall not want any money there. Jesus meant that we should be trying all the time to live so that at last we may live in heaven. In heaven we shall have more things to make us happy than all the money in the world can buy.

He said to the people, "You cannot obey God and Satan, too." We cannot do this, because if we obey God we will do right, but if we obey Satan we will do wrong. We cannot obey both, and, therefore, we must choose which one to obey.

He told His disciples not to judge other people; He meant that we should be careful how we find fault with others and blame them. Perhaps they never did the thing we blame them for. If we are certain that they did, perhaps they didn't mean any harm. We cannot see their hearts and tell how they felt while they were doing it; only God can tell that. Perhaps He does not blame them. How often we ourselves do the very thing we blame others for doing. Jesus said we should first stop doing wrong ourselves. Then we will be able to tell others of their faults.

He told the people who were listening to Him on the mountain, and He tells you and me, that whatever we want other persons to do to us, we must do to them. If we want them to treat us kindly and justly, we must treat them kindly and justly, too.

He said, "Strive earnestly to go in at the narrow gate, for wide is the gate and broad is the way that leads to destruction."

Not everyone, Jesus said, who called Him Lord or Master would be taken up to heaven. Only those would be taken who obeyed His Father in heaven. Many persons who had not obeyed God would come to Him at the judgment day. They would call Him "Lord, Lord," and would say they had worked for Him and had taught other persons about Him. But He would tell them they had never truly been His disciples. He would send them away.

He told a story about two men, each of whom built a house. One chose a rock to build his house upon. When it was done, a great storm came and beat against it. But the rain could not move the rock, nor could the wind blow it away. The house stood firm, and the storm did it no harm. The other man built his house in a place where there was nothing but sand. The storm came against it, also. The rain washed the sand away from underneath the house, and the wind blew against it. The house fell and was destroyed.

Jesus said that people who listened to His teaching and did what He taught them were like the wise man who built his house upon the rock. But those who listened to His teaching and would not do what He taught them were like the foolish man who built his house upon the sand.

Some Parables

Jesus and his disciples went about the country teaching the people and healing the sick.

One day He spoke a parable to the people. A parable is a story which has a meaning to it and which helps us to understand and remember something we are learning. Jesus told the people this parable so that they might know how foolish and wicked it was for them to put their trust in riches.

He said, "There was a rich man who had fields and vineyards. When harvesttime came, he gathered his fruits. There were so many that his barn would not hold them. He said to himself, 'What shall I do? I have no room for all my fruits.' He answered himself by saying, 'I will pull down my barns and build larger ones for all my fruits and my goods. Then I will say to myself, now I can eat and drink and be merry, for I have enough riches laid up to last me for many years.'

"But when the rich man had spoken these words, God said to him, 'Thou foolish man, this night thou must die. Who then shall have those things which thou hast laid up for many years?'

"And so it will be with all those persons who care only to lay up riches for themselves in this world, but do not care to please God. Death will come when they are not expecting it. They will have to leave their riches for others and will have to go away to a world where nothing has been laid up for them."

Jesus told His disciples not to be afraid because they were poor. They should not fear that they might be without food to eat and clothes to wear.

"Think of the birds," He said. "They do not sow seed in the fields or reap grain and carry it to the barn to lay it up there. Yet they always have enough to eat, because God feeds them. God cares even more for you.

"Look at how the flowers grow. They do not work like men to make raiment for themselves, and yet they are more beautifully clothed and have brighter colors than Solomon when he was king of Israel. If God gives such beautiful clothing to the flowers, which are of so little value that one day they are growing up in the field and the next day they are cut down and burned, He will be more careful to clothe you. Therefore, do not be anxious about things to eat, and to drink, and to wear, for your heavenly Father knows that you need these things.

"Seek first to obey Him and be His children. Then He will give all these things to you."

Once when Jesus walked by the seaside, great multitudes came to Him. He went into a boat and sat down to teach them. The multitude stood on the shore and listened to His words.

He told them a parable. "A farmer went out in the field

to sow his seed. He scattered the seed by handfuls over the ground. Some of the seed fell upon the hard, beaten path that ran along the edge of the field. The birds flew down and ate the seed. Some fell upon stony places where there was only a little earth. There it quickly grew up above the ground. But because there was not enough earth to make larger roots, in a few days it withered away. Some of the seed fell along the side of the field where briars and weeds were growing. The briars grew up and choked it. But the rest of the seed fell upon good ground that had been plowed and made ready to receive it.

"The rain fell on it and watered it, and the sun shone upon it. It sprang up and bore grain, a hundred times as much as the farmer had planted."

When Jesus was alone, His disciples came and asked Him to explain this parable to them. He answered that the seed meant the words which He preached. Some of those who heard the words did not understand what He said, nor care to remember them. Then Satan made them think of other things and took His words out of their hearts as quickly as the birds ate up the seed that fell on the pathway. Some who heard Him remembered His words and tried for a little while to obey them. But it was only for a little while. As soon as trouble came, these people ceased trying and forgot the words. This was the seed that fell on the stony ground.

Some heard Jesus preach and were glad to hear what He said. But afterward they went away to their homes and paid more attention to their houses, their riches, and their pleasures than they did to the things He had taught them. This was the seed that fell among thorns.

But there were some people who listened to all that Jesus taught. They remembered it and tried every day to do as He told them. This was the good seed that took root and grew and bore a hundred times as much as the farmer had planted.

185

Jesus spoke a parable about a mustard seed. A mustard seed is among the smallest of seeds. Yet when a man plants it in the ground, it grows to be the largest of herbs, and the birds come and lodge in its branches. So it is, Jesus said, with our love for God. At first it seems very small. If we are truly His children, however, it will go on growing stronger and greater until we love Him more than we love anyone else. Then we will try harder in all that we do to please Him.

Jesus told the people about a merchant who was looking for pearls to buy. He went to every person who had any to sell, hoping to find some that would suit him. At last he found one that was larger and more beautiful than any he had ever seen before. Its price was so great that he did not have enough money to buy it. Therefore, he went away and sold everything he had, so that he might come back and buy that one precious pearl.

This is the way persons feel who want their sins forgiven. They cannot be happy until they are forgiven. They are willing to give up every sinful pleasure and everything that offends God, so that they may come to Him and ask Him to forgive their sins for them.

Jesus Heals the Sick

ONCE WHEN JESUS went into Capernaum, one of the rulers of the synagogue came to Him. Kneeling down at His feet, the ruler begged Him, "My little daughter is sick and ready to die. I pray Thee come and lay Thy hands on her, that she may live."

Jesus went with him, and so did His disciples. Many people followed after Him and crowded around Him.

Among them was a woman who had suffered for twelve years from a disease which no physician could cure. She had given the physicians all the money she had, yet she was no better. When she heard that Jesus was near, she said to herself, "If I can but touch His garment, I shall be made well." So she followed in the crowd behind Him and touched Him. As soon as she had done it she felt that her sickness was cured.

Then Jesus turned toward the people that followed Him and said, "Who touched Me?"

His disciples answered, "Thou seest the multitude pressing against Thee, and askest Thou, 'Who touched Me?' " Jesus looked around to see who had done this thing. When the woman saw that He knew it and that she could not be hid, she came to Him, trembling. Falling down at His feet, she told all the people why she had touched Him and how in a moment she was made well.

Jesus said to her, "Daughter, be not afraid. Because thou hadst faith in Me, thou art healed."

While He was speaking to the woman, there came to the ruler of the synagogue a messenger, saying, "Your daughter is dead. Therefore, do not trouble the Master any further."

Jesus said to him, "Fear not. Have faith, and she shall live."

They went to the ruler's house where Jesus saw the people weeping and wailing greatly. He said to them, "Why do you weep? The child is not dead, but sleeping." He meant that she would soon rise up from the dead like one who waked out of sleep.

They would not believe Him, and they laughed Him to scorn. Jesus took three of His apostles—Peter, James, and John—and the father and mother of the child and went into the room where she lay.

He took her by the hand and said, "I say to thee, arise."

The child, who was twelve years of age, rose and walked. Those who saw it wondered greatly.

As Jesus went away from the ruler's house, two blind men followed Him and cried after Him, "Thou son of David, have mercy on us."

They called Him this because He was descended from King David.

Jesus said to them, "Do you believe that I am able to make you well?"

188

They answered, "Yes, Lord."

Then He touched their eyes, and immediately they were able to see.

Jesus said to them, "Tell no man what I have done for you." But when they left Him they told the people through all that country how He had healed them.

They brought to Him a dumb man who could not speak because an evil spirit had entered into him. Jesus cast out the evil spirit, and the man spoke. All the people wondered and said, "We have never seen such things done before in the land of Israel."

One day Jesus said to His disciples, "Come, let us go some place apart, where you may rest awhile." They entered a boat and sailed to the other side of the Sea of Galilee so that they might be alone.

When the people heard of it, they followed Jesus and his disciples on foot, walking around by the side of the sea and coming to the place where Jesus was. He talked to them there throughout the day.

In the evening His apostles said to Him, "This is a desert place where there is nothing to eat. The day is now passed. Send the people away that they may go into the villages and buy themselves food."

Jesus said, "They need not go away. Give them something to eat."

The apostles answered, "Shall we go and buy two hundred pennyworth of bread and give it to them to eat? Even this would not be enough for each one of them to take a little."

He said to them, "How many loaves have you? Go and see."

When they knew, they answered, "Five loaves and two small fishes."

Jesus commanded His apostles to make all the people sit down in groups on the green grass. He took the five loaves and the two fishes and looked up to heaven and thanked God for them. Then He broke the loaves in pieces and gave them to the apostles. The fishes also He divided among them. The apostles gave them to the multitude. As they were being given to the people, Jesus made those few loaves and fishes increase so that there was enough for them all.

When they had eaten, He said, "Gather up what is left, so that nothing be lost."

They gathered twelve basketfuls of the pieces which were left. Those that had eaten were about five thousand men.

When the people saw this great miracle which Jesus had done, they wanted to make Him their king. But He left them and went up on a mountain alone to pray. He sent the apostles away in the boat to go across the sea toward Capernaum.

In the evening the apostles were rowing in the middle of the sea. Jesus was alone on the shore, and from there He could see them toiling, for the wind was against them and the waves were rough and stormy. In the night He went out to them, walking on the sea.

When they saw Him, they were afraid. "It is a spirit," they cried out with fear.

But Jesus said to them, "Be not afraid. It is I."

Then Peter answered out of the boat, "Lord, if it be Thou, bid me come to Thee on the water."

Jesus said to him, "Come."

Peter came out of the boat and walked on the water to go to Jesus. When he heard the noise of the wind and saw the great waves dashing around him, he was afraid and began to sink. "Lord, save me," he cried.

Immediately Jesus stretched out His hand and caught Peter. He said to him, "O thou of little faith, why didst thou doubt?"

When Jesus and Peter entered the boat, the wind was still. In a moment the boat reached the point of land

190

where the apostles wanted to be.

Then they worshipped Him, saying, "Truly, Thou art the Son of God."

As soon as they reached the shore, the people knew Him. They ran through the country and began to carry those who were sick to the place where they heard He was. Wherever He went in villages or cities, they laid the sick in streets and begged that they might touch Him, even if it were only His garment. As many as touched Him were made perfectly well.

Two More Parables

ONE DAY AS the disciples and Jesus were walking, Jesus told them a parable. He said, "There was a king who wanted to take an account of the money which his servants owed him. One servant was brought who owed him a very great sum—as much as ten thousand talents. Since he had nothing to pay with, the king commanded that he and his wife and his children should be sold as slaves, and that the purchase price might be paid for the debt. The servant fell down on his knees before the king and prayed that he would have patience with him until he could earn the money or get it from those who owed it to him. 'Then,' he said, 'I will pay you all.' When the king saw the servant's distress, he pitied him and was kind to him and forgave the debt altogether.

"That same servant went out and found one of his fellow

servants who owed him only a hundred pence. He caught the fellow servant by the throat and said, 'Pay me what you owe.' The fellow servant fell down at his feet and begged him, 'Have patience with me, and I will pay you all.' But he would not have patience. Instead, he cast him into prison, to be kept there till he should pay the debt.

"The king's other servants, who saw what he had done, were very sorry, and they told the king. The king called the servant to him and said, 'O wicked servant. I forgave you all your debt because you asked me. Should you not, also, have pitied your fellow servant as I pitied you?' The king was greatly offended and sent the servant to be punished."

On another day while He was teaching the people, a lawyer stood up to ask Him a question. "Master, what must I do to be saved?" he asked.

Jesus said, "What does God's law command thee to do?"

The lawyer answered, "Thou shalt love the Lord thy God with all thy heart, and with all thy soul, and with all thy strength, and with all thy mind; and thy neighbor as thyself."

Jesus said, "Thou hast answered right. Do these things and thou shalt be saved."

But the lawyer wanted to excuse himself, and so he said, "Who is my neighbor?"

Then Jesus spoke this parable. "A certain man went down from Jerusalem to the city of Jericho. On the way he got among thieves, who stripped him of his clothing and wounded him and went away, leaving him half-dead. While he lay on the ground too weak to rise, by chance a priest came along. As this priest was a minister and a teacher of God's law, we might suppose that he would have shown kindness to the wounded man. But, instead, he crossed over to the other side of the road and pretended that he did not see the wounded man. And after the priest, a Levite came. He also was one of those who attended to

God's worship at the temple. Yet when he looked at the man, he passed on as the priest had done, without offering to help him.

"After the priest and the Levite had gone, a Samaritan came to the place where the wounded man lay. When the Samaritan saw him he pitied him and went to him and bound up his wounds, pouring in oil and wine to make them heal. Then he lifted him up and, setting him on his own beast, took him to an inn and nursed him there.

"As he was leaving the next day he took out money and gave it to the owner of the inn, saying, 'Take care of him. Whatever more you spend for him after I am gone, when I come again I will pay you.' "

After He had told this parable, Jesus said to the lawyer, "Which of these three do you think was neighbor unto him who fell among thieves?"

The lawyer answered, "The one that showed kindness to him."

Then Jesus said to him, "Go and do thou likewise."

Jesus Teaches the People

WHEN JESUS CAME to a village called Bethany, which was a little way from Jerusalem, a woman named Martha asked Him to her house. She had a sister named Mary, who, when Jesus had come, sat down at His feet so that she might listen to what He taught. Because she had all the work to do, Martha was displeased with her sister. She said to Jesus, "Lord, dost Thou not care that Mary has left me to do the work alone? Bid her, therefore, that she come and help me."

Jesus answered, "Martha, Martha, you are troubled about many things; yet only one thing is needful. Mary has chosen that, and it shall never be taken away from her." He meant that Mary had chosen to learn about God and His will for her. This knowledge, Jesus said, is far more important than household tasks.

Jesus taught His disciples what they should say when they prayed to God. He said, "When you pray, say, 'Our Father, who art in heaven, hallowed be Thy name. Thy kingdom come, Thy will be done on earth as it is in heaven. Give us this day our daily bread. And forgive us our trespasses, as we forgive those who trespass against us. And lead us not into temptation, but deliver us from evil. For Thine is the kingdom, and the power, and the glory forever. Amen.' "

Jesus told His disciples to ask God for those things that they needed, and God would grant them. He said, "If one of your children should ask you for bread, would you give him a stone? Or if he asked for a fish, would you give him a serpent? If you, then, who are sinful men, know how to give good things to your children, how much more certain is it that your heavenly Father will give the Holy Spirit to them that ask Him."

Jesus said that God would give us the Holy Spirit because that is the best gift He can give us. It is the Holy Spirit who comes into our hearts and changes them into new hearts and so makes us God's children.

Great multitudes often came to hear Jesus. But He said to them that, although a man might come and listen to His words, yet if he did not in his heart care more for Him than for anyone else in the world, he could not be His disciple. If he did not take up his cross—that is, deny himself to do only what is right, as Jesus Himself did—he could not be His disciple.

"For which of you," He asked, "who intends to build a house does not first sit down and count how much it will cost and find out whether he has enough money to build it? Lest after he has begun and built only a little way, he may have to stop, and all that see it mock him, saying, 'This man began to build but was not able to finish.' Or what king who is going to make war against another king does not first consider how large an army his enemy has,

196

lest his own army be too small to fight against it?"

Jesus said that any man who wanted to follow Him must think first of what he would have to do. Unless he was willing to give up all that he had if Jesus asked him to do so, he could not be His disciple.

Then the tax collectors and other men who were sinners came near to hear Him. When they saw this, the scribes and Pharisees found fault with Jesus. "He keeps company with wicked men and eats with them," they said.

But Jesus answered, "Which of you, having a hundred sheep, if he lose one of them, does not leave all the rest and go after that which is lost till he finds it? And when he has found it, he takes it up on his shoulders and carries it home, rejoicing. He says to his neighbors and friends, 'Rejoice with me, for I have found my sheep which was lost.'

"Or what woman who has ten pieces of silver, if she lose one piece, does not light a candle and sweep the house and look carefully until she finds it? When she finds it, she says to her friends and her neighbors, 'Rejoice with me, for I have found the piece which was lost.' "

In these parables Jesus meant to teach the scribes and Pharisees that the tax collectors and sinners who came to hear Him were like the lost sheep and the lost piece of silver because they were wicked. Yet He would not for this reason send them away. Instead, he would look for them and encourage them to come to Him so that He might teach them to repent. He said that even the angels in heaven were glad whenever one of those wicked men repented and began to serve God.

He spoke another parable. "There was a man who had two sons. The younger one said to his father, 'Father, give me my share of the riches which you have laid up for your children.' His father gave him his share. Not many days afterward, the younger son took all that he had and went away into a far country. There he wasted what his father had given him. When he had spent everything, there came a famine in that land, and he began to want bread to eat. He hired himself to a man of that country, who sent him out into his fields to feed swine. He would have been glad to have some of the coarse food which the swine ate, but the man did not give it to him.

"After he had suffered awhile, he said to himself, 'In my father's house there are many hired servants who have plenty to eat and more than they want, while I stay here starving with hunger. I will arise and go to my father and will tell him I have sinned against God and done wickedly to him and do not deserve to be called his son. I will ask him to let me come back to his house and be treated as one of his hired servants.'

"So he left that country to go back to his father. While he was still a good way off, his father saw him coming. He pitied him and ran out to meet him and put his arms around his neck and kissed him. Then the son said to him, 'Father, I have sinned against God and done wickedly to you. I do not deserve to be called your son.'

"But his father said to the servants, 'Bring out the best robe and put it on him and put a ring on his hand and shoes on his feet. Bring the fatted calf and kill it, and let us eat and be merry, for my son, who had left me, has come back again. He was lost, and now he is found.' And they began to be merry.

"Now, the elder son was out in the field. When he came near the house, he heard music and dancing. He called one of the servants and asked him what these things meant. The servant answered, 'Your brother is here. Your father has killed the fatted calf because he has come back safe and sound.' This made the elder son angry and he would not go in. His father came out to him and begged him. But he answered his father, 'For a great many years I have served you and obeyed your commandments. Yet you never gave me a kid that I might make a feast for my

friends. Yet as soon as this wicked son returned, you killed for him the fatted calf.' The father answered, 'My son, I have always loved you. Everything I have is the same as though it were yours. Yet it is right that we should be glad and rejoice, for your brother had left us, and he has come back again. He was lost, and now he is found.' "

In this parable Jesus taught the proud scribes and Pharisees, who blamed Him for preaching to sinners, that God loved those sinners and was willing to forgive them, if they would only cease doing evil and obey Him.

Jesus spoke a parable to those persons who thought themselves more righteous than others. He said, "Two men went up to the temple to pray; one of them was a Pharisee and the other a publican. The Pharisee chose a place where the people would see him. There he stood up proudly and prayed in this way: 'God, I thank Thee that I am not like other men, who are unjust and who take more than belongs to them. I thank Thee that I am not a sinner like this publican. I fast twice in the week. I give to the priests and Levites a tenth part of all that I get.' The publican knew he was wicked, and he was sorry for it. He stood where he hoped no one would notice him and, bowing down his head, he beat upon his breast in great distress, saying, 'God be merciful to me, a sinner.' "

Jesus told those who listened to Him that this publican went back to his home forgiven more than the Pharisee. "For," He said, "everyone who is proud and thinks much of himself shall be put down. He who is humble and confesses his sin shall be raised higher."

The people brought little children to Jesus so that He might put His hands on them and bless them. His disciples found fault with those who brought them and wanted to send the children away. But Jesus was much displeased at His disciples and said, "Let the little children come unto Me and forbid them not, for of such is the kingdom of heaven."

He meant that only those persons who are humble and loving, like little children, will come into His kingdom. He took the little children up in His arms and put His hands upon them and blessed them.

Jesus and His disciples journeyed together. He told them they were going up to Jerusalem. When they should come there, He said, all those things would happen to Him which the prophets had spoken. He would be mocked and scourged and spit upon. He would be crucified, and on the third day He would rise again. But because the apostles still expected Jesus to set up an earthly kingdom, they could not understand Him when He spoke of those things.

Other Stories About Jesus

WHEN JESUS AND the apostles came to Jericho a great number of people followed Him. A blind man named Bartimeus sat by the wayside begging. Hearing the multitude, he asked what it meant. They told him that Jesus of Nazareth was passing by.

As soon as he heard this he began to cry out with a loud voice, "Jesus, thou son of David, have mercy on me."

When the people heard him crying out, they told him to be silent. But he cried much more, "Thou son of David, have mercy on me."

Jesus stood still and commanded the blind man to be called. And they called to him, "Be of good comfort, rise. He calls for you."

Then the blind man rose up in haste and threw away his outer garment so that he might go quickly to Jesus.

Jesus said to him, "What wilt thou have Me do for thee?"

The blind man answered, "Lord, that Thou wouldst give me my sight."

Jesus said, "Because thou hast faith, thou art made well."

Immediately he could see. He followed Jesus, praising God for what had been done to him.

There was in Jericho a man named Zaccheus. He was the chief tax collector, and he was rich. As Jesus passed through the streets of the city, Zaccheus tried to see who it was, but he could not, for the crowd was large and he was a little man. So he ran on ahead and climbed into a sycamore tree.

When Jesus came to the place, He looked up and saw Zaccheus and said to him, "Zaccheus, make haste and come down, for today I must stay at thy house." Zaccheus made haste and came down, and he received Jesus into his house.

Now, the tax collectors, who took the people's money for the king, were often unjust and cruel men. It is very likely that Zaccheus was like this before Jesus came to his house. But when Jesus came he believed that God had sent Him. He listened to His teaching and obeyed His words.

Zaccheus stood up before all the people who were there and told Jesus that he would be unjust no more. He would be kind to the poor, he said, and he would give them half of all the money he had. If he found he had taken anything that did not belong to him, he would give back four times as much.

When Jesus saw how Zaccheus repented of his sins and obeyed what He taught him, He told Zaccheus that all his sins were forgiven.

The Jews found fault with Jesus for going to the house of a publican, and they said that He had gone to stay with a man who was a sinner. Jesus told them that He had come into the world to go among sinners, so that He might teach them to repent and save them from being punished for their sins.

The Entrance Into Jerusalem

THE FEAST OF the Passover was near, and many of the people went up to Jerusalem to keep it. They looked for Jesus there. As they stood in the courts of the temple, they said to one another, "Will He not come to the feast?" For the chief priests and the Pharisees had commanded that if any man knew where Jesus was, he should tell them.

On His way to Jerusalem, when He was near the Mount of Olives, Jesus said to two of His disciples, "Go into the village which is near you, and you shall find there a colt tied, on which no man has yet ridden. Loosen him and bring him to Me. If any man asks, 'Why do you this?' you shall say, 'Because the Lord has need of him.' "

The two disciples found the colt, as Jesus had said. As they were loosening him, the owners asked, "Why do you loosen the colt?"

They answered, "The Lord has need of him." The owners let the disciples take the colt, and they brought him to Jesus. The disciples put their garments upon the colt, and Jesus rode on him.

As He rode toward the city a great multitude took off their outer garments and spread them in the way so that He might ride over them. They did this to honor Him.

The multitudes that went before Him and that followed after Him cried with a loud voice, "Hosanna! Blessed is He that has come to us, sent by the Lord."

Jesus knew, however, that although they now praised Him, many of them did not love Him in their hearts. He knew that in a few days they would be crying out to crucify Him. As He came near to Jerusalem, He wept when He thought of the sufferings that were coming upon the Jews. Their enemies would bring an army, He said, and make a camp around the city and besiege it and destroy it. Every house would be thrown down, so that not one stone would be left standing. Although He had come from heaven to save them, the Jews would not believe in Him and were going to put Him to death.

When He came into Jerusalem, He went up to the temple. The blind and the lame were brought to Him, and He healed them.

When the chief priests and the scribes saw the miracles that He did, and heard the children in the temple praising Him and crying out, "Hosanna," they were displeased.

One day soon after His arrival in Jerusalem, a Pharisee, who was also a teacher of the laws of Moses, came to Jesus and asked Him a question. He said, "Master, which is the first of all God's commandments?"

Jesus answered, "Thou shalt love the Lord thy God with all thy heart, and with all thy soul, and with all thy mind. This is the first and great commandment.

"And the other one which is like it is: Thou shalt love thy neighbor as thyself."

Then Jesus said, "On these two commandments hang all the law and the prophets." He meant that all the other commandments in the Bible come from these two. If we obey the first, we shall do our duty to God; if we obey the last, we shall do our duty to our neighbor. In this way we shall do everything that the Bible commands us to do.

Jesus called the scribes and Pharisees hypocrites because they loved to sit in the chief seats in the synagogues and make long prayers there, in order that the people might see and praise them. At the same time they were unjust to other persons and cruel to the poor. For these things, Jesus said, they should receive greater punishment at the judgment day.

Jesus sat in the court of the temple where the boxes were placed into which the people cast money which they gave to buy sacrifices. Many persons who were rich gave a great deal of money. There came a poor widow who gave two mites, which were less than a penny. Jesus called His disciples to Him and told them that what the poor widow gave seemed more to God than all that the rich men had given. They, Jesus said, had much left for themselves, because they gave out of their riches, while she had nothing left for herself, because she gave all that she had.

The Last Days

WHEN JESUS CAME to Bethany, the town where Mary and Martha and Lazarus lived, they made Him a supper there.

Mary took a pound of costly ointment, which was called spikenard, and, bowing down at the feet of Jesus, she anointed them with it and wiped them with her hair. The house was filled with the sweet smell of the ointment.

One of His apostles, named Judas Iscariot, said, "Why was not this ointment sold for three hundred pence, and the money given to the poor?" Judas did not say this because he cared for the poor, but because he was a thief. He carried the bag in which the money was kept, and he wanted to take it for his own.

But Jesus said to him, "Let her alone. Why do you find fault with her? She has done a good work. You have the poor with you always and you may do them good whenever you wish, but you will not have Me always."

Jesus said to His disciples that wherever His gospel should be preached over the whole world, this thing that Mary had done to Him should be told so that it might be remembered of her.

Judas Iscariot went to the chief priests and said to them, "What will you give me if I bring you to the place where He is, so that you may take Him?"

They promised to give him thirty pieces of silver. From that time on he tried to find Jesus alone so that he might betray Him to them.

The Last Supper

THE DAY HAD come when the Jews made ready for the feast of the Passover. To do this, each man took a lamb to the temple and killed it, as a sacrifice, before the altar. The priests burned its fat on the altar, and the rest of the lamb the man took to his home. There it was roasted, and he and his family ate of it in the night, for, as we have read, the feast of the Passover was eaten in the night.

Jesus and His apostles were going to keep this feast together, and the apostles came to Him and asked at what place they should make it ready.

He answered, "Go into Jerusalem and there you will meet a man carrying a pitcher of water. Follow him into the house where he is going, and say to the man who lives there, 'The Master wants thee to show us the chamber where He shall come to eat the feast of the Passover with His disciples.' The man will show you a large upper room. There make ready the feast."

The disciples did as Jesus commanded, and the man showed them the room where they were to eat. They made the feast ready there.

In the evening Jesus came with His twelve apostles and sat with them at the table.

He said to them, "I have greatly desired to eat this Passover with you before I die, for I say unto you, I will not anymore eat of lamb that has been sacrificed until I Myself have been sacrificed for the sins of the people."

The apostles did not understand Him when He spoke of being sacrificed for the people. They still thought that He was going to set up an earthly kingdom and that the time for Him to do this was coming near.

They began to dispute among themselves, as they had done before, about which of them should be greatest in that kingdom.

Jesus told them that among the people of the world, those who were great ruled over the rest. "But," He said, "it shall not be so with you. Whoever among you will be the greatest, let him be the most humble. The one who will be chief, let him be as if he were the servant of all."

Jesus asked them which was the greatest, the person who ate at the table or the one who served Him while He ate.

"Yet," He said, "I am among you as the one who serves."

He arose from the table and laid aside His outer garment. He took a towel and girded Himself with it. After that He poured water into a basin and began to wash the disciples' feet and wipe them with the towel.

Peter did not wish Jesus to wash his feet as though Jesus were his servant. When Jesus came to him, Peter said to Him, "Lord, wilt Thou wash my feet?"

Jesus answered, "Thou dost not understand why I do it now, but thou shalt know afterward."

Peter said, "Thou shalt never wash my feet."

Jesus answered him, "If I wash thee not, thou canst not be one of My disciples."

Then Peter said, "Lord, wash not my feet only, but also my hands and my head."

Jesus said to him, "He that is washed needs only to wash his feet."

After He had washed their feet and put on the garment which He had laid aside, He came to the table again. He said to them, "Do you know what I have done unto you? You call Me Master and Lord, and you say well, for so I am. If I, then, your Lord and Master, have washed your feet, you ought to wash one another's feet, for I have given you an example that you should do as I have done to you."

As they ate of the Passover, Jesus said to them, "Verily, I say unto you, one of you shall betray me."

The disciples were filled with sorrow, and they looked on one another wondering of whom He spoke. One of the disciples whom Jesus loved was near to Him. Peter motioned to him that he should ask Jesus of whom He spoke. The disciple leaned on Jesus' breast and said to Him, "Lord, who is it?"

Jesus answered, "It is he to whom I shall give a piece of bread when I have dipped it in the dish."

When He had dipped the bread He gave it to Judas Iscariot. After that, Satan went into Judas. Jesus said to him, "What thou art going to do, do quickly."

No man at the table knew what Jesus meant by these words. Because Judas carried the bag in which the money was kept, some of them thought that Jesus commanded him to go and buy those things of which they had need, or that he should give something to the poor.

Judas left the house where Jesus and the apostles were.

When he was gone, Jesus said to them, "I will be with you only a little while. Before I leave you I give a new commandment to you. It is that you love one another; as I have loved you, so shall you also love one another. If you have love one to another, everyone will know that you are My disciples!"

Jesus told the apostles that they would all be tempted to leave Him that night.

Peter answered, "Though all the rest shall leave Thee, I never will, for I am ready to go to prison and be put to death with Thee."

Jesus said, "I tell thee, Peter, that this night, before the cock crows twice, thou shalt three times deny that thou knowest Me."

But Peter answered confidently, "Though I should die with Thee, I will not deny Thee." And so they all said.

As they were eating together, Jesus took bread and blessed it. He broke it in pieces and gave it to His apostles, saying, "Take and eat, for this is My body which is broken for you." He meant that the bread was like His body, and represented it, because His body was soon to be broken and crucified and offered up on the cross for them.

Then He took some wine in a cup and when He had thanked God, He gave it to them and they all drank of it. He said to them, "This wine is My blood, which is shed for the forgiveness of sins."

He meant that the wine was like His blood, and represented it, because His blood was very soon to be shed, like the blood of the sacrifices at the altar, so that all who believed in Him might have their sins forgiven.

He commanded His apostles to meet together, after He should be put to death, and to eat the bread and drink the wine in the same way that He had shown them. As often as they did it, they were to remember Him. We call this Communion, or Lord's Supper.

As they sat at the table Jesus talked with His apostles. He

told them not to be troubled because He was to be taken away from them. He was going to heaven, He said, to make a place for them. Afterward He would come and take them, so that where He was they might be.

He said to them, "Obey My commandments, for it is he who obeys My commandments that loves Me. Whoever loves Me, My Father will love."

He promised them that His Father would send the Holy Spirit into their hearts to make them remember and understand everything He had told them. The Holy Spirit would also teach them what they should teach others. It would stay with them, and be their Comforter, while He was away from them.

Jesus said, "I am the vine and ye are the branches." He meant that He was like a vine and the apostles were like the branches growing out of the vine. The good branches, which bore fruit, He said, His Father took care of and made stronger, so that they would bear more fruit. The bad branches which bore no fruit were cut off and thrown into the fire. If the apostles wanted to bear fruit—that is, if they wanted to do the good works that Jesus told them to do—they must keep on loving and obeying Him. Without His help they could do nothing that was good.

He told the apostles that He had chosen them to bear fruit and do good works among the people. They must remember what He had told them: that the people would not love them for doing these things, but would hate them and persecute them.

"Now," He said, "you have sorrow, because I am to be taken away from you, but after I have risen from the dead, I will see you again, and then you shall have joy."

He commanded them when they asked anything from God, to ask it in His name and for His sake. They had never before prayed in this way, but now they were to do it. God would answer the disciples when they prayed in Jesus' name, because Jesus was the one who had borne the punishment for their sins.

Then Jesus lifted up His eyes to heaven and prayed for His disciples and for all those who would hear the words that His disciples preached, and believed in Him. He prayed that they might be kept from sin and might love one another. He said that He wanted them to be with Him in heaven, where they could see the glory which His Father had given Him.

After these things Jesus and His apostles sang a hymn together. Then they went out from the house.

Jesus Is Betrayed

JESUS AND HIS disciples walked until they came to the
Mount of Olives, which was a little way from Jerusalem. There they went into a garden, called the Garden
of Gethsemane.

Jesus said to His apostles, "Sit ye here while I go yonder
and pray."

He went a little way from them and kneeled down and
prayed. Because He was being punished for our sins and
knew that in a few hours He would be crucified, He was in
agony. His sweat seemed like great drops of blood falling
down to the ground. An angel came and comforted Him.

When He rose up from prayer and went back to His
disciples, He found them sleeping. He said to them, "Why
sleep ye? Arise and pray, lest you be tempted to do wrong."
He went away again and prayed. When He returned He

found them sleeping. When He came the third time, He said, "Rise up and let us be going. Behold, he who will betray Me is coming near."

Judas had been watching when Jesus went to the garden. Because it was night and only a few of His disciples were with Him, Judas thought it the best time to betray his Master. Therefore, he went to the chief priests and elders and told them where Jesus was. They gave him a band of men to go with him and take Jesus. Now, Jesus knew that Judas was bringing the men to the garden, but He did not flee. He waited to let them take Him, because the time had come for Him to die. While He was speaking with His apostles and telling them that the one who would betray Him was near, Judas came with the band of men carrying swords and staves and lanterns.

Judas had said that he would give them a sign. "The one that I shall kiss is He. Take Him and hold Him fast."

He came to Jesus and said, "Master, Master." Then he kissed Him.

Jesus said, "Judas, dost thou betray Me with a kiss?"

The men laid their hands on Jesus and took Him. When the apostles saw them take Jesus, they said to Him, "Lord, shall we fight them with the sword?" Peter, having a sword, drew it and struck a servant of the high priest, cutting his ear.

But Jesus said, "Put thy sword back into the sheath. Might I not now pray to My Father that He would send Me quickly many thousands of angels to fight for Me and save Me from death? But how then could the words of the prophets come true, which say that I am to die for the people?"

Then Jesus touched the servant's ear and healed it. He said to the men that took Him, "Have you come with swords and staves to take Me, as though I were a thief? I sat daily with you, teaching in the temple, and you did nothing to Me."

All His apostles were afraid. They left Him and fled.

The men took Jesus to Caiaphas, the high priest. In the high priest's palace were gathered together all the chief priests, scribes, and elders, and Jesus was brought before them. Peter had followed Jesus, a good way off, hoping that no one would know him. He came into the high priest's palace and sat down among the servants near a fire, for he wanted to see what would be done.

A young woman came to him and said, "Thou wast with Jesus of Galilee." But Peter denied it. And when he went out on the porch, the cock crowed, as Jesus had said it would.

There another maid saw him. She said to those who stood by, "This fellow also was with Jesus of Nazareth."

Again Peter denied it. "I do not know the man," he said.

After a while, one of the servants of the high priest, who was a relative of the man whose ear Peter had cut off, said, "Did not I see you with Him in the garden?"

Peter denied it again, and the second time the cock crowed. Jesus turned and looked at Peter. Then Peter remembered the words which Jesus had spoken to him. When he thought of it, he went out and wept bitterly. From that time on, Peter never denied knowing Christ.

The high priest asked Jesus about His disciples and about the gospel that He preached. Jesus answered, "I taught in the synagogue and in the temple, where the Jews always go. In secret have I taught nothing. Why askest thou Me? Ask those who heard Me what I said to them. They know what I said."

When He had finished speaking, one of the officers who stood by struck Him with the palm of his hand. "Dost Thou dare to answer the high priest so?" he demanded.

Jesus said to him, "If I have spoken evil, tell those who should punish Me, but if I have spoken well, why dost thou strike Me?"

Now, the chief court of the Jews, which tried persons who disobeyed the law, met in a room near the temple. It was called the Council of the Sanhedrin, and it was made up of seventy men. The high priest and the chief priests and many of the scribes and elders were among the members. These men were the rulers of the Jews, and they punished in different ways persons who had disobeyed the law of Moses. Whenever they wanted to punish anyone by putting him to death, they had to ask permission of the Roman governor, for the Jews, being servants to the Romans, were not allowed to put anyone to death without the governor's consent.

As soon as it was morning the men brought Jesus before the council. There the chief priests and scribes and elders tried to find false witnesses that would speak against Him.

At last two false witnesses came forward. They said, "This fellow said, 'I am able to destroy the temple and build it up again in three days.' "

Jesus was silent and did not answer them.

Then the high priest arose and said, "Answerest Thou nothing?"

Jesus did not reply.

The high priest said, "I ask Thee to tell us whether Thou are the Christ, the Son of God."

Jesus answered, "I am. I say unto you, that hereafter you shall see Me sitting on the right hand of God and coming back to earth again in the clouds of heaven."

Then the high priest rent his clothes and said, "What need have we of any more witnesses against Him? You have heard the wicked blasphemy He speaks. What do you say His punishment should be?"

The men in the council said He should be put to death. Then they spat in His face and mocked Him. When they had blindfolded Him they struck Him with the palms of their hands and called out, "Tell us, Thou Christ, who it is that struck Thee?"

221

After they had bound Him, the council rose and led Jesus to Pontius Pilate, the Roman governor. When they brought Him into Pilate's house they began to accuse Him before the governor. "We found this fellow teaching the Jews to rebel against the Romans, forbidding them to pay tribute to the emperor, and saying that He Himself is Christ, a king."

Pilate asked Him, "Art Thou a king?"

Jesus answered, "I am, but My kingdom is not of this world, for then would My servants fight to save Me from the Jews."

Pilate said to the chief priest and to the Jews who had brought Him, "I find no fault in this man."

They were even more fierce and cried out, "He stirs up the people to do wrong throughout all Judea, from Galilee to Jerusalem."

When Pilate heard them speak of Galilee, he asked if Jesus came from there. When they told him that He had come out of Galilee, he sent Jesus to Herod, who was governor over that part of the land.

When Herod saw Jesus, he was glad, for he had long wanted to see Him because he had heard many things about Him. He hoped also to see some miracle done by Him. Herod asked Jesus many questions, but Jesus did not answer. The chief priests and scribes stood by and bitterly accused Him. Then Herod and his soldiers made sport of Jesus. They mocked Him and put on Him a purple robe, because He had said He was a king and kings dressed in purple. Afterward Herod sent Him back to Pilate to be questioned again.

Pilate called together the Jews, with the chief priests and rulers, and said to them, "You have brought this man to me as one that stirs up the people to do wrong. But I, having questioned Him before you, have found no fault in Him. Neither has Herod. Nothing for which He ought to die has been proved against Him."

Now, at the time of the feast of the Passover every year, if any of the Jews were shut up in prison for disobeying the Romans, the Roman governor set one of them free. He allowed the Jews to say which prisoner it should be in order to please them and make them more willing to let him rule over them. There was at this time in prison a Jew named Barabbas, who had been put there for murder. The people began to ask the governor to do for them as he had always done before and set one of the prisoners free.

Pilate said, "Which one shall it be? Barabbas or Jesus, who is called Christ?" He knew that they had brought Jesus to be punished only because they hated Him.

While Pilate was speaking with them, his wife sent word to him, saying, "Do no harm to that just man, for I have been much troubled this day in a dream concerning Him."

But the chief priests persuaded the Jews to ask that Barabbas might be set free. Pilate said to them, "What, then, shall I do with Jesus, who is called Christ?"

They all said, "Let Him be crucified."

Pilate said, "Why, what evil has He done?"

They cried out with loud voices, "Crucify Him!"

When Pilate saw that he could not persuade them to ask for Jesus, he took some water and washed his hands before the people. "I am not to blame for the death of this just man. See you to it," he said.

All the people answered by saying, "Let the blame be on us and on our children."

Washing his hands did not take the blame from Pilate, however. The sin was in his heart. When he knew that Jesus was innocent, he gave Him up to be crucified, for fear the Jews might be offended and demand that someone else be their governor.

In those days, before they crucified a man, the Romans used to scourge him. He was stripped to the waist. His

223

hands were bound to a low post in front of him, which made him stoop forward. While he stood in this way, he was cruelly beaten with rods. Pilate, therefore, took Jesus and scourged Him.

Then the soldiers who were to put Him to death led Him into a room in the governor's palace and called together the whole band of soldiers to which they belonged. There they took off His outer garment, and to mock Him, as Herod had done before, they put on Him a purple robe. They plaited a wreath of thorns and put it on His head instead of a crown. And, instead of a golden scepter, such as kings held, they put a reed in His right hand.

Then they bowed down before Him, pretending He was a king, and said to Him, "Hail, King of the Jews." Then they spat upon Him and, taking the reed, they struck Him upon the head.

After He had suffered all these things, Pilate hoped that the Jews would be willing to let Him go. He spoke to them again, saying, "I bring Him out to you, to tell you once more that I find no fault in Him."

Then Jesus came out before the multitude, wearing the crown of thorns and purple robe. Pilate said to them, "Behold the man!"

But when the chief priests and officers saw Him, they cried out, "Crucify Him, crucify Him!"

Pilate said to them, "Take Him yourselves, then, and crucify Him, for I find no fault in Him."

The Jews answered, "We have a law, and by our law He ought to die, because He said that He was the Son of God."

When Pilate heard them say this, he was even more afraid to put Jesus to death. He said to Jesus, "From what place didst Thou come?" Jesus gave him no answer.

Then Pilate said, "Wilt Thou not speak to me? Knowest Thou not that I have power to crucify Thee and power to let Thee go?"

Jesus answered, "Thou canst do only that to Me which God will let thee do."

The emperor of Rome, whose name was Caesar, was a jealous and cruel man. Pilate feared him. When the Jews saw that Pilate wanted to set Jesus free, they cried out, "If you let this man go, you are not Caesar's friend because He said He was king instead of Caesar."

After they said this Pilate was afraid to let Jesus go, lest the Jews might tell Caesar. Therefore, he gave Him to them to be crucified as they wished.

When Judas saw that Jesus must die, he was afraid of what he had done. He returned the thirty pieces of silver to the chief priests and elders, saying, "I have sinned, because I have betrayed one who is innocent."

They answered, "What is that to us? See to that yourself."

Judas threw down the thirty pieces of silver in the court of the temple and went away and hanged himself.

The chief priests took the silver pieces and said to one another, "It is against the law to put them into the treasury at the temple, because they were paid for a man who is to be put to death." Therefore, they bought with them the potter's field to bury strangers in.

The soldiers took off the purple robe from Jesus and put His own clothes on Him. Then they led Him away to put Him to death. A man named Simon, whom they met coming out of the country, helped Him carry the cross. There followed a great multitude of people, who mourned and wept for Him. Turning to them, Jesus told them that they should not weep for Him but for themselves and their children, because of the sorrows that were coming on the Jews.

The Crucifixion

THE SOLDIERS BROUGHT Jesus to a place called Calvary, which was a little way outside the gates of Jerusalem. There they nailed His hands and His feet to the cross and crucified Him.

While they were crucifying Him, Jesus prayed for them, saying, "Father, forgive them, for they know not what they do!" He meant that they did not know how great their sin was in crucifying Him, the Son of God.

With Jesus were two thieves, one on His right hand and the other on His left, who were being crucified, also.

Now, persons who were crucified did not die at once; they lived many hours, hanging on the cross. So, although He was crucified in the morning, Jesus hung in agony until the afternoon. The soldiers who had crucified Him sat down and watched Him. They took His garments and divided them among themselves; for His coat they cast lots.

Upon the cross, above His head, Pilate had these words written: JESUS OF NAZARETH, THE KING OF THE JEWS. Many of the Jews read these words, for the place where He was crucified was near the city. Many of them felt no pity for Him. They shook their heads at Him, saying, "If Thou be the Son of God, come down from the cross."

The chief priests and the scribes also mocked Him and said, "He trusted in God; let God help Him now if He will have Him."

One of the thieves who were crucified with Him said wickedly to Jesus, "If Thou art the Christ, save Thyself and us."

But the other thief answered him, "Do you not fear God, seeing you also are soon to die? We deserve to die for our wicked acts, but this man has done nothing wrong."

Then he said to Jesus, "Lord, remember me when Thou comest into Thy kingdom."

Jesus answered him, "Today shalt thou be with Me in paradise."

From the sixth hour until the ninth hour there was a darkness over all the land; that is, from twelve until three o'clock, the time when the sun usually shines brightest, it was dark over all the land. God sent that darkness because His Son was being put to death by wicked men.

About the ninth hour Jesus cried out with a loud voice, "My God, My God, why hast Thou forsaken Me?"

When one of the men who was standing near heard Him cry, he took a sponge and filled it with vinegar and lifted it up on a reed to His mouth and gave Him to drink. When Jesus had taken the vinegar, He said, "It is finished." He meant that the work which He had come to do, and the punishment which He had come to bear for us, were finished. He bowed His head and died.

At that moment the curtain, called the veil, which

227

hung in the temple was torn in two from top to bottom. The earth shook. The rocks were broken in pieces, and graves were opened.

When the Roman soldiers who were watching Jesus saw these things, they feared greatly and said, "Surely this man was the Son of God."

The Resurrection

A T THE PLACE where Jesus was crucified there was a
garden, and in the garden was a new sepulcher in
which no one had ever been buried. It belonged to a
rich man named Joseph who came from the city of
Arimathea.

Joseph was a disciple of Jesus, though he had never
before let it be known because he was afraid of the Jews.
After Jesus was dead, Joseph went to Pilate and
begged for His body. Pilate commanded that the body
should be given to him. Joseph took it down from the
cross and wrapped it in new, fine linen and laid it in the
sepulcher. A great stone was rolled to the door and left
there.

Mary Magdalene and Mary, the mother of the apostle
James, were sitting near the sepulcher and saw where

Jesus was laid. They went away to rest during the Sabbath.

After Jesus was buried, the chief priests and the Pharisees came to Pilate and said, "Sir, we remember that while that deceiver was yet alive, He said, 'After three days I will rise again.' We pray you, therefore, that the sepulcher may be watched and made safe until the third day, lest His disciples should come in the night and steal Him away and then go and tell the people He has risen from the dead."

Pilate answered, "You shall have soldiers to guard the sepulcher. Go and make it as secure as you can." So they went and made certain the sepulcher was secure, setting soldiers to watch it and sealing the stone that was rolled to the door.

That night the angel of the Lord came down from heaven and rolled back the stone from the door and sat upon it. His face was bright like lightning, and his garments were as white as snow. The soldiers trembled for fear of him. They left the sepulcher and went into the city again.

Early in the morning, as soon as it began to be light, Mary Magdalene and the other Mary and Salome came to the sepulcher, bringing spices and ointment to put on the body of Jesus, in the manner in which the Jews prepared the dead for burial.

As they were coming, they said one to another, "Who shall roll away the heavy stone for us from the door of the sepulcher?"

When they came near, they found the stone was rolled away. Entering the sepulcher, they saw an angel clothed in a long white garment. They were greatly frightened.

He said to them, "Be not afraid. You seek Jesus who was crucified. He is not here. He is risen. See the place where they laid Him. Go tell His disciples that He is risen from the dead and that He will go before you into Galilee. There shall you see Him."

They went out quickly and fled from the sepulcher, with fear and yet with great gladness, and ran to bring His disciples word.

On the way Jesus met them and said to them, "Rejoice." They came and held Him by the feet and worshipped Him.

He said to them, "Be not afraid. Tell My brethren that they go into Galilee. There shall they see Me."

The women told these things to the eleven apostles and to the disciples who were with them. When Peter and John heard what the women said, they came in haste to the sepulcher. John outran Peter and came first to the sepulcher. Stooping down and looking in at the door, he saw the linen clothes which Jesus had worn, lying there.

When Peter came, he went into the sepulcher and saw the linen clothes and the napkin which had been wrapped about the head of Jesus. The napkin was not with the linen clothes, but folded together in a place by itself. Then John went in, also, and he saw and believed that Jesus was risen. Before that time they had not understood the words which He had spoken to them while He was yet alive, saying that after three days He would rise from the dead. The apostles went away to their own homes.

Now, after Jesus was risen some of the soldiers who had guarded the sepulcher went to the chief priests and told them what had happened. The chief priests and elders gave them a large sum of money and said to them, "Go and tell the people that His disciples came at night and stole Him away while you slept. If the governor should hear of it and want to punish you for sleeping [the Roman soldiers were put to death if they slept while on guard], we will persuade him to pardon you."

So the soldiers took the money and did as the chief priests told them.

On the first day of the week when Jesus was risen from the dead, two of His disciples were walking together to a village called Emmaus, which was about seven miles from Jerusalem. As they walked, they talked with one another of all the things that had been done. While they were talking, Jesus came near and went with them. But He was changed so that they did not know Him.

He said to them, "What is it that you are saying to one another as you walk?"

One of them, whose name was Cleopas, said to Him, "Art Thou a stranger in Jerusalem? Hast Thou not heard of the things which have happened there in these days?"

He said, "What things?"

They answered, "Concerning Jesus of Nazareth, who was a prophet and did great miracles before all the people; how the chief priests and the rulers have taken Him and set the children of Israel free from the Romans. Today is the third day since He was put to death. Some of the women who belong to our company and who went early to the sepulcher have astonished us by saying that His body was not there and that they saw a vision of angels who told them He was alive. Some of the men who were with us went afterward to the sepulcher and found it was as the women had said. But they saw Him not."

Then Jesus told the two disciples that the things which had happened in Jerusalem seemed strange to them because they did not understand what the prophets had written. "For was it not to be expected," He asked, "from what the prophets had said about Christ, that He should be put to death and afterward should rise from the dead and go up to heaven?" Then He explained to them what was written about Himself in the Scriptures. But still the two disciples did not know Him.

As they came near the village to which they were going, He walked on, as though He would leave them and go farther. But, supposing Him to be some traveler, they said to Him, "Come and stay with us tonight, for it is near evening and the day has almost gone."

He went with them into the house. While they were at supper Jesus took bread and, after He had thanked God for it, He broke it and gave it to them. As He did this they knew Him. Suddenly He was gone out of their sight.

Then they said to one another, "Were not our hearts interested while He talked with us and explained to us what the prophets have written?" They rose up that same hour and went to Jerusalem and found the eleven apostles gathered there.

The two disciples told them how they had seen Jesus and talked with Him, and how they had known Him as He was breaking the bread.

While they were speaking, Jesus Himself stood in the midst of them and said, "Peace be unto you." They were frightened, for they thought it was a spirit.

He said to them, "Why are you troubled? And why does fear come into your hearts? Look at My hands and My feet; touch Me, and see that it is I, Myself, for a spirit has not flesh and bones as you see Me have."

When He had spoken these words He showed them His hands and His feet. The marks of the nails were in them. They could hardly believe what they saw. He said to them, "Have you here any food?" They gave Him a piece of a broiled fish and a honeycomb, and He took them and ate before them.

He said to them, "I told you while I was yet with you that all those things must be fulfilled which are written in the Scriptures about Me."

Then He made the apostles understand those parts of the Scriptures which said that He should die for the people and rise again from the dead. They knew all of this, but they had not been able to understand it until now.

Jesus said to them, "Thus it was written about Me, and therefore it was needful for Me to suffer death and to rise up from the dead on the third day, so that the people of all nations might be told how I have died for them. If they will repent and believe in Me, they shall have their sins forgiven. And you, my apostles, are the ones who know of these things. On that account I send you forth to tell the nations about them. Go you, therefore, into all the world and tell this good news to every creature. Whoever believes in Me and is baptized shall be saved; but he that believes not shall be lost."

Thomas, one of the apostles, was not with the others when Jesus appeared. When they told him, afterward, that they had seen the Lord, Thomas answered, "Unless I shall see in His hands the marks of the nails, and thrust my hand into the wound that the spear made in His side, I will not believe it was He."

After eight days the apostles were again gathered together. Thomas was with them this time. Jesus came and stood in the midst and said to them, "Peace be unto you." Then He said to Thomas, "Reach out thy finger and touch My hands, and reach out thy hand and thrust it into My side. Be not faithless, but believe that I have risen again."

When Thomas heard His voice and knew that it was Jesus, he said, "My Lord and my God."

Jesus said to him, "Thomas, because thou hast seen Me, thou hast believed; but I say unto thee, blessed are those who are willing to believe even though they have not seen Me."

Later Jesus showed Himself again to His disciples at the Sea of Galilee. There were together Peter, Thomas, Nathaniel, James, John, and two other disciples.

Peter said to them, "I am going a-fishing."

They answered, "We will go with you." They went into a boat and sailed out on the sea, but that night they caught nothing. When morning came, Jesus stood on the shore, but the disciples did not know it was Jesus.

He said to them, "Have you any food?"

They answered, "No."

He said, "Cast the net on the right side of the boat and you shall find some."

When they did as He commanded, they were not able to draw up the net because of the multitude of fish that were caught in it.

Therefore, that disciple whom Jesus loved said to Peter, "It is the Lord."

When Peter heard it was the Lord he fastened his fisherman's coat around him and cast himself into the sea, so that he might hasten to the shore. The other disciples came in the boat, dragging the net. As soon as they had come to land they saw a fire burning there, with fish laid upon it, and bread.

Jesus said to them, "Bring some of the fish which you have caught."

Peter drew the net up on the land. It was full of great fish—a hundred and fifty and three. Yet, although there were so many, the net was not broken.

Jesus said to them, "Come and eat."

None of the disciples dared ask Him, "Who art Thou?" for they knew that it was the Lord. This was the third time He had shown Himself to them since He had risen from the dead.

At another time He met them on a mountain in Galilee, where He had told them to go that they might see Him. When they saw Him they worshipped Him. He said to them, "God has given Me all power, both in heaven and in earth. Go you, therefore, and preach the gospel to the people of all nations, baptizing them in the name of the Father, and of the Son, and of the Holy Ghost, teaching them to do all those things that I have commanded you."

Not only to His disciples did Jesus show Himself. He was seen also by more than five hundred of those who believed in Him.

When forty days had passed since He had risen from

the dead, He met His apostles again at Jerusalem. When He had talked with them and commanded them to wait there until the Holy Spirit should be sent upon them, He led them out as far as Bethany. He lifted up His hands and blessed them. While He blessed them, He was taken from them and carried up into heaven; He went into a cloud out of their sight.

While they looked toward heaven as He went up, behold, two angels in white garments stood by them. They said, "Ye men of Galilee, why do you stand gazing up into heaven? This same Jesus who is taken up from you into heaven shall come down again, in the clouds, as you have seen Him go up into heaven."

The Apostles Continue Preaching

T HE DISCIPLES DID as Jesus commanded. They went out to preach to all people. Christ had given them also the power to make the sick well and the lame to walk again.

Peter and John went up together to the temple at the hour of prayer. A poor man who had been lame ever since he was born was carried every day by his friends and laid at the gate of the temple, called the Beautiful Gate, so that he might ask alms, or gifts, of those who came up to worship. This man, seeing Peter and John about to go into the temple, asked them for alms.

Fixing his eyes upon him, Peter said, "Look on us."

The man looked, for he supposed they would give something to him. Then Peter said, "I have no silver and gold, but what I have I will give you. I tell you, in the name of Jesus Christ of Nazareth, to rise up and walk."

Peter took him by the right hand and lifted him up. Immediately his feet and ankle bones were made strong. Leaping up, he stood and walked with them into the temple.

All the people saw him. They knew that it was he who sat to ask for alms at the Beautiful Gate of the temple. They were filled with wonder at what had been done, and they ran together to the place where the apostles stood.

Peter spoke to them, saying, "You men of Israel, why do you wonder at this? Or why do you look so earnestly on us, as if we had made this man walk? It is Jesus who has given us the power to make him well. Therefore, brethren, repent and believe in Jesus, that when He shall come again at the judgment day, your sins may be forgiven."

Now, there was among the Jews a sect, or society of men, called Sadducees. They did not believe there would ever be any judgment day, or that the dead would ever rise from their graves. Some of these Sadducees belonged to the Council of Sanhedrin.

While Peter and John were speaking at the temple, the Sadducees came there. They were angry because the apostles preached about Jesus and the resurrection. They put Peter and John in prison to keep them till the next day, for it was now evening. Yet many of the people who heard Peter and John believed, so that the number of them was about five thousand.

The next day all the council met together. When Peter and John were brought in, they asked them, "By what power did you heal the lame man?"

Peter answered, "You rulers of the people, and elders of Israel, if you ask us about the good deed done to the lame man, and how he was healed, we tell you it was by the power of Jesus of Nazareth, whom you crucified, that he was made well. For though you counted Jesus as nothing while He was on earth, yet God has made Him to be ruler over us all. Neither is there any other person in the

239

world who can save us from being punished for our sins."

When the rulers saw that Peter and John were poor and unlearned men, and yet were bold and without fear in speaking before them, they were astonished. Seeing the man who had been healed standing near them, they could not deny what the apostles had done. They commanded Peter and John to go for a little while out of the council, while they talked among themselves. They said to each other, "What shall we do to these men, for that they have done a great miracle is known to all the people in Jerusalem, and we cannot contradict it. So that the news of it may spread no farther, let us say that we will punish them if they preach anymore to the people."

Then they called Peter and John and commanded them not to teach about Jesus. Peter and John answered, "Whether it is right for us to obey you more than God, you yourselves may judge. We cannot help teaching the people about Jesus, and telling them of the things that we have heard Him speak and seen Him do."

After the rulers had threatened again to punish them, they let them go because they could not prove any evil.

Peter and John went to the other apostles, and to the disciples who were with them, and told of what the rulers had said. Then they all prayed together, saying, "Lord, help us, that we may not be afraid to preach the gospel. Give us power to do miracles also in Jesus' name."

When they had prayed, the place where they were gathered together was shaken. In this way God let them know that He heard their prayer and would give them that for which they asked.

They went out and preached again to the people with boldness, not fearing what the rulers could do to them. Many heard them and believed, and all who believed met together, helping and loving one another. As many as had houses or land sold them and brought the money to the apostles that they might give alms to the poor.

The Conversion of Saul

SAUL, WHO WAS also called Paul, was full of anger and hatred against the disciples of Jesus. He went to the high priest at Jerusalem and asked for letters to the rulers of the synagogues in the city of Damascus, so that he might go to that city and, if he found any disciples there, bind them with fetters and bring them to Jerusalem to be punished.

The high priest gave him the letters he asked for, and he started on his journey to Damascus. As he came near that city, suddenly there shone around him a great light from heaven, and Jesus appeared to him.

Saul was afraid, and he fell down on the ground.

He heard a voice saying, "Saul, Saul, why dost thou persecute Me?"

Saul said, "Who art Thou, Lord?"

The voice answered, "I am Jesus, whom thou persecutes." It was Jesus speaking to Saul. He meant that when Saul persecuted His disciples, he persecuted Him.

Then Saul, trembling and astonished, said, "Lord, what wilt Thou have me do?"

The Lord said, "Arise and go into the city, and it shall be told thee what thou must do."

The men who were with Saul stood silent. They heard the voice, but they did not see Jesus. Saul saw nothing, for the light had blinded him. Those with him led him by the hand and brought him into Damascus. He was three days without sight, and all that time he neither ate nor drank.

At that time there was living in Damascus a disciple named Ananias.

The Lord said to him, "Arise and go into the street which is called Straight. Ask at the house of Judas for a man named Saul. He is now praying to Me and has seen thee in a vision, coming to him and putting thy hand on him, that he may receive his sight."

Ananias answered, "Lord, I have heard many speak of this man, and of the great evil he has done to Thy people in Jerusalem. He has come here with letters from the chief priests, letting him bind in fetters all who believe in Thee."

The Lord said, "Go, as I have told thee, for I have chosen him to preach My gospel to the Gentiles and to kings and to the children of Israel."

Ananias obeyed and went into the house of Judas. Putting his hands on Saul, he said, "Brother Saul, the Lord Jesus, who appeared to you as you were coming to Damascus, has sent me to put my hands on you, that you may receive your sight and be filled with the Holy Ghost."

Immediately Saul's eyes were opened and he could see. He rose up and was baptized. After he had eaten some food his strength came to him again. Then he stayed with the disciples who were in Damascus. He went into the synagogues and preached about Christ to the people, telling them that Jesus was the Son of God.

But all who heard him were amazed. They said, "Is not this the man who persecuted those in Jerusalem who believed, and who came here that he might bind the disciples and carry them to the chief priests to be punished?"

Yet Saul preached more and more earnestly and proved to the Jews at Damascus that Jesus was the Savior; although they would not believe, the Jews could not deny what he said.

After many days had passed, the Jews, being filled with anger, talked with one another about some way of killing Saul. They watched by day and by night, hoping to take him when he should go out through the gates of the city. The disciples heard of it, however, and took him by night and let him down in a basket from a window that was over the wall, so that he escaped out of Damascus and afterward went to Jerusalem.

Saul continued to serve Jesus faithfully. Later he was known as Paul, the Apostle, who wrote the letters to the Romans, the Corinthians, and many other people. These letters are now books in the New Testament.

Peter and Cornelius

THERE WAS A man in the city of Cesarea named Cornelius. He was a centurion in the Roman army. He was not a Jew, yet he was a good man. He loved God and taught his family to love Him. He gave alms to the poor and prayed to God always.

About the ninth hour of the day, Cornelius saw in a vision an angel coming to him, saying, "Cornelius."

When he saw the angel he was afraid. "What is it, Lord?" he asked.

The angel answered, "God has heard thy prayers and seen the alms which thou hast given. Now send men to Joppa for a man named Peter, who is staying in the house of Simon, a tanner, which is by the seaside. When he has come to thy house, he will tell thee what thou ought to do."

After the angel had gone, Cornelius called two of his servants who waited upon him, and also a soldier who loved God, and whom he kept with him continually.

When he told them what the angel said, he sent them to Joppa.

The next day Peter, who did not know they were coming, went up on the housetop to pray about the sixth hour. As he prayed, he grew very hungry and wanted to eat. Then he had a vision. He saw the sky above him open, and something like a great sheet, held up at four corners, was let down to the earth in front of him. In this sheet were all kinds of wild beasts and creeping things and birds of the air. There came a voice, saying, "Rise, Peter; kill and eat."

We have read how Moses commanded the children of Israel not to eat any of the animals that were called unclean. Some of these animals were in the sheet. When the voice told Peter to kill and eat, he answered, "I cannot do it, Lord, for I have never eaten anything that is forbidden or unclean."

Then the voice spoke again. "What God has made clean, do not thou call forbidden or unclean." These words were spoken three times, and then the sheet was lifted up and taken toward heaven again.

It was God who sent the vision to Peter. The reason He sent it was this: The Jews thought that because God had chosen them for His people they were better than other nations, and that Jesus came to save them alone. They called other nations unclean and did not want to preach the gospel to them.

God taught Peter that this was wrong. The animals that he saw in the vision represented those other nations, and God intended in this way to show Peter that he should not call them unclean anymore, nor refuse to teach them, but should preach to them just as he preached to the Jews. God had made those nations as well as the Jews, and Jesus had been sent to save the other nations, also.

While Peter was wondering what the vision could mean, the servants of Cornelius came to Simon's house and stood before the gate and asked if Peter was there.

Then the Holy Spirit spoke to Peter. "Behold, three men are looking for thee. Arise and go with them, without fear, for I have sent them."

Peter went down to the men and said to them, "Behold, I am he whom you seek. For what reason have you come?"

They answered, "Cornelius, the centurion, who is a just man and who loves God, and is well thought of by all the Jews, was told by a holy angel to send for you to come to his house, that he might hear the words which you would speak."

Peter called the men into Simon's house, and kept them that night. The next day he went with them, and some of the disciples who lived at Joppa went, also.

When they came to Cesarea, Cornelius was expecting them, and he invited his relatives and his friends to be with him. As Peter entered into his house Cornelius fell down and worshipped him. Peter said to him, "Stand up, for I am only a man like yourself."

Peter went in with him and found many persons gathered together who, like Cornelius, were not Jews, but Gentiles. Peter said to them, "You know that the Jews say it is wrong for them to make friends with the men of other nations, because the Jews think themselves better and call others common and unclean. But God has taught me, in a vision, not to call the men of other nations common or unclean. Therefore, I came to you as soon as you sent for me. Now I ask, for what reason did you want me to come?"

Cornelius answered, "Four days ago I was fasting and praying in my house, and, behold, an angel stood before me in bright clothing and said, 'Cornelius, God has heard thy prayers and has seen thy kind acts to the poor. Send,

246

therefore, to Joppa for a man named Peter. He is staying in the house of Simon, a tanner, by the seaside. When he comes, he will tell how thee and all thy family can be saved.' Immediately then I sent for you, and you have done kindly to come. Now, therefore, we are all met together to hear what God has commanded you to say."

Peter said to them, "Truly I see that God does not choose one nation to be His people more than another, but in every nation those persons who love Him and do what is right, He takes for His children. You have heard of the words that are preached to the children of Israel about Jesus—how God sent Him into the world, and how He went about doing good. Yet the Jews took Him and put Him to death. God raised Him up again on the third day, and showed Him to us, His apostles, who did eat and drink with Him after He had risen. He commanded us to go and preach to the people, and tell them that God has appointed Him to be the Judge of all men. He is the one of whom the prophets said that all those who believe in Him shall have their sins forgiven."

While Peter was speaking, the Holy Ghost came upon Cornelius and the other Gentiles who were with him. The Jews who had come with Peter from Joppa were astonished, for they thought that God did not care for the Gentiles. Now they saw that He sent His Holy Spirit upon them, and they heard the Gentiles speaking in other languages which they had never known before, the Holy Spirit giving them power to do so.

Peter said, "Ought not these men be baptized, to whom the Holy Ghost has been sent as well as to us?" He commanded them to be baptized in the name of Jesus.

The apostles and disciples at Jerusalem heard that Peter had gone to visit Cornelius and his friends at Cesarea. When Peter returned to Jerusalem they found fault with him, saying, "You went into the house to visit men who are Gentiles and did eat with them." Peter then told them of all that had happened to him—how God had taught him by the vision that he was to preach the gospel to the Gentiles, also, and had commanded him to go with the men whom Cornelius sent. He said, "While I was preaching to Cornelius and his friends, the Holy Ghost came upon them as He did upon us, who are Jews, at the day of Pentecost. Therefore, as God sent His Spirit upon them, what was I, that I should oppose Him?"

When the apostles and disciples heard these things, they ceased to blame Peter. They gave thanks, saying, "God has given the Gentiles new hearts, that they may be saved as well as we."

About that time, Herod, the king, began to persecute the Christians. He killed James, one of the apostles. When he saw that this pleased the Jews greatly, he took Peter, also, and put him in prison, setting soldiers to watch over him, by night and by day, so that he should not escape. Herod intended after the feast of the Passover to bring Peter out to the people and put him to death. While Peter was in prison, prayer was made continually by the church in Jerusalem for him.

On the night before he was to be brought out, Peter was sleeping between two soldiers. He was bound with two chains that were fastened to the soldiers' hands, so that if he moved they would be sure to know it.

Behold, an angel came to him, and a light shone in the prison. The angel touched Peter's side and wakened him saying, "Rise up quickly."

The soldiers did not even waken.

The chains fell off from Peter's hands, and the angel said to him, "Dress thyself and put on thy sandals and follow me." Peter followed him, but he thought it was only a dream. When they had passed the guard of soldiers they came to the iron gate that led into the city. It opened to them of its own accord. They went out and walked on through the first street. There the angel left him.

When Peter had time to think of what had been done he said to himself, "Now I know surely that the Lord has sent His angel to save me from Herod and from the Jews, who expected to kill me."

He went to the house of Mary, the mother of the disciple whose name was Mark, where many Christians were gathered together praying. As Peter knocked at the gate, a young woman named Rhoda came to listen. When she heard his voice, she was so full of gladness that she forgot to open the gate for him, but ran back and told those who were in the house that Peter was there.

They said to her, "You are mad; Peter is in prison." Yet she declared even more earnestly that it was he. They said, "It must be his spirit."

Still Peter continued knocking. When they opened the door and saw him, they were astonished. Motioning with his hand that they should be still, he told them how the Lord had brought him out of prison. He said, "Go tell these things to the other apostles." And he left them and went to another place.

As soon as it was morning, the soldiers wondered where Peter had gone. When Herod called them to him and questioned them, they could not tell what had become of Peter. Herod commanded that they should be put to death.

Paul Shipwrecked

AT ONE TIME Paul was taken prisoner and was sent with other prisoners to Rome. A Roman centurion was in charge of them.

After sailing slowly many days, they reached a place called Fair Havens on the island of Crete.

Since it was winter, and the time for storms on the sea had come, Paul said to the men on the ship, "Sirs, I see that while we are on this voyage there will be great danger, not only to the ship, but also to our lives."

But the master of the ship did not believe what Paul said, and did not think that Fair Havens was a good harbor to stay in for the winter. He was determined to leave it and try to reach a place called Phenice. When there came a wind that blew softly from the south, the sailors thought they would be able to do this. Therefore, they left Fair Havens and sailed out on the sea again.

Soon there arose a fierce wind which beat against the ship. When the sailors could steer no longer, they let the ship go wherever the wind might drive her.

They came near an island called Clauda. There they could hardly save the little boat that was fastened behind the ship from being washed away. When they had taken it up out of the water, they wound cables about the ship, underneath and all around it, to keep it from breaking to pieces. The next day, being greatly tossed by the tempest, they threw out into the sea some of the cargo to make the ship lighter and save it from sinking. The following day they threw over all the ropes and sails that could be spared.

When the wind kept on blowing for many days, and they could see neither sun, nor moon, nor stars, because of the dark clouds that covered the sky, the people gave up all hope, thinking they would surely be lost.

After they had eaten nothing for a long time, Paul stood up among them and said, "Sirs, you should have listened to me and stayed at the island of Crete. Then you would not have come into this great danger. Yet now I beg you be not afraid, for there shall be no loss of any man's life among you, but only of the ship. For this night the Lord sent His angel, who spoke to me, saying, 'Fear not, Paul. Thou shalt come safely to Rome and be brought before Caesar. For thy sake, God will save the lives of all the men who are with thee in the ship.' Therefore, sirs, be cheerful, for I believe what the angel told me. Yet we shall be wrecked on some island."

On the fourteenth night, as the ship was driven along by the wind, the sailors thought they were near some land. After they had measured the depth of the water, they found that it was so. Fearing they would strike on rocks at the bottom of the sea, they dropped four anchors out of the ship to keep it from being driven any farther, and then wished for morning. Then, supposing the ship would soon be broken to pieces, the sailors let down the little boat into the water, intending to escape in it and leave the others to be drowned.

Paul said to the centurion, "Unless these sailors stay in the ship, the rest cannot be saved." The sailors cut off the ropes that held the boat, and let it float away.

When it was nearing morning, Paul begged them all to take something to eat. "This is the fourteenth day since the storm came upon us, and you have eaten hardly anything. Therefore, I pray you, take some food, that you be not made sick, for there shall not the least harm happen to any one of you."

When he had said this, he took bread and thanked God for it before them all and began to eat. Then were they all cheerful and ate with him. There were altogether two hundred and seventy-six persons in the ship. After they had eaten, they threw into the sea some of the wheat with which the ship was loaded, to lighten it.

When it was day they saw the shore, though they could not tell to what land they had come. Seeing a creek a little way off, they determined, if they were able, to push the ship into it. After they had taken up the anchors and hoisted the sail, they steered toward that place. Before they reached it, however, the ship ran aground. The forepart was held fast on the bottom of the sea and could not be moved, and the hinder part was broken by the great waves that dashed against it. The soldiers advised the centurion to have the prisoners killed, for fear some of them might escape. But the centurion, wishing to save Paul, forbade them to do the prisoners any harm and commanded that those who could swim should first cast themselves into the sea and get to the shore. The rest, some on boards and some on broken pieces of the ship, came afterward. Thus they all safely reached land.

They found that the place was an island called Melita.

PAUL SHIPWRECKED

The people of the island showed them great kindness and kindled a fire for them, because of the rain that was falling and because of the cold.

Paul gathered a bundle of sticks and laid them on the fire, but after he had done so a poisonous snake came out of the heat and fastened on his hand. When the people of the island saw it hanging upon his hand, they said among themselves, "No doubt this man is a murderer, who, though he escaped drowning in the sea, is yet punished by the bite of the snake for the evil he has done." But Paul shook off the snake into the fire and felt no harm.

They looked at him a long while, expecting that his arm would swell or that he would fall dead suddenly. When they saw that no harm came to him, they changed their minds and said that he was a god.

The chief man of the island, whose name was Publius, invited Paul and those who were with him to his house. They stayed three days and they were treated kindly there.

Now, the father of Publius was sick of a fever, and Paul laid his hands on him and made him well. When he had done this, others on the island who were sick came and were healed. They showed their gratitude by giving to Paul and his friends presents of such things as they needed.

After three months, the centurion took Paul and the other prisoners into a ship that had been waiting at the island till the winter was over. They sailed to the city of Puteoli, where they stayed seven days with some disciples who lived there. Then they journeyed by land toward Rome. When the Christians at Rome heard Paul was coming, they went out to meet him at a place called the Three Taverns. After he had seen them, he gave thanks because he had been saved from so many dangers. He felt in his heart that God would still take care of him.

When they came to Rome, the centurion gave the prisoners into the care of the captain of the guard, but

Paul was allowed to live in a house by himself with the soldier who watched over him, although the chains that he had worn so long were not taken off from him. After three days he sent for the chief men among the Jews who lived at Rome and said to them, "Men and brethren, though I have done no wrong to the Jews, nor disobeyed the laws which Moses spoke to our fathers, yet the Jews at Jerusalem gave me a prisoner to the Romans, who, when they examined me, would have let me go, because I had done nothing for which I deserved to die. But when the Jews still wanted to kill me, I asked to be taken before Caesar. Therefore, I have sent for you to come so that I might see you and speak with you, for it is because I believe in that Savior about whom the prophets have written that I am bound with this chain."

When he said this the Jews answered, "We have had no letters sent to us about you. Neither do these Jews who have come from Jerusalem speak any harm of you. We would like to hear what it is you preach, for we know that everywhere these Christians have lived they have been harshly spoken against."

So after they had appointed a day, many of the Jews came to Paul's house and he taught them from morning till evening, explaining what the prophets had written about Jesus. Some believed the things he spoke, and some did not believe. When they differed among themselves, he told them that the prophet Isaiah had spoken the truth when he said that, although a message from God should be brought to the people of Israel, they would not listen to it, because their hearts were wicked and they did not want to be His children. Therefore, Paul told them that the gospel which the Jews refused to believe should be preached to the Gentiles. They, he said, would obey it.

Paul stayed two years in Rome. He welcomed all those persons who came to hear him, and he taught them about Jesus without fear, for no man ever tried to prevent him.